Dogs 101: A Guide to American Kennel Club Breed Groups, Vol. 6 - The Non-Sporting Group

Jacob Cleveland

Six Degrees Books. This book was created and put into distribution by a team of dedicated editors and subject matter experts using open source and proprietary publishing tools. The name "Six Degrees Books" is indicative of our desire to make it easy for people to find valuable, but not readily apparent, relationships between pieces of digital content and compile that information into helpful and interesting books.

Curation is King. One of the advantages to the way we publish books is that our content is up to date and written by dedicated subject matter experts from all over the world. By adding a layer of careful screening and curatorial attention to this, we are able to offer a book that is relevant, informative and unique.

We are looking to expand our team: If you are interested to be a Six Degrees editor and get paid for your subject matter expertise - please visit www.sixdegreesbooks.com.

Contents

Articles

References

Breed Groups (dog)

A **Breed Group** is a categorization of related breeds of animal by an overseeing organization, used to organize the showing of animals. In dogs, kennel clubs define the *Breed Groups* and decide which dog breeds are to be included in each *Breed Group*. The Fédération Cynologique Internationale *Breed Groups* are used to organize dogs for international competition. *Breed Groups* often have the names of, and are loosely based on, ancestral dog types of modern dog breeds.

Recognized Breed Groups

International

The Fédération Cynologique Internationale makes sure that dogs in its 84 member countries can compete together, by establishing common nomenclature and making sure that pedigrees are mutually recognized in all the member countries. So internationally, dog breeds are organized in ten groups, each with subsections according to breed type and origin.

- **Group 1 - Sheepdogs and Cattle Dogs (except Swiss Cattle Dogs)**
- **Group 2 Pinscher and Schnauzer - Molossoid Breeds - Swiss Mountain and Cattle Dogs**
  - Section 1: Pinscher and Schnauzer type
  - Section 2: Molossoid breeds
  - Section 3: Swiss Mountain and Cattle Dogs
- **Group 3 Terriers**
  - Section 1: Large and medium-sized Terriers
  - Section 2: Small-sized Terriers
  - Section 3: Bull type Terriers
  - Section 4: Toy Terriers
- **Group 4 Dachshunds**
- **Group 5 Spitz and Primitive types**
  - Section 1: Nordic Sledge Dogs
  - Section 2: Nordic Hunting Dogs
  - Section 3: Nordic Watchdogs and Herders
  - Section 4: European Spitz
  - Section 5: Asian Spitz and related breeds
  - Section 6: Primitive type
  - Section 7: Primitive type - Hunting Dogs
  - Section 8: Primitive type Hunting Dogs with a ridge on the back

- **Group 6 Scenthounds and Related Breeds**

  - Section 1: Scenthounds
  - Section 2: Leash (scent) Hounds
  - Section 3: Related breeds (Dalmatian and Rhodesian Ridgeback)

- **Group 7 Pointing Dogs**

  - Section 1: Continental Pointing Dogs
  - Section 2: British and Irish Pointers and Setters

- **Group 8 Retrievers - Flushing Dogs - Water Dogs**

  - Section 1: Retrievers
  - Section 2: Flushing Dogs
  - Section 3: Water Dogs

- **Group 9 Companion and Toy Dogs**

  - Section 1: Bichons and related breeds
  - Section 2: Poodle
  - Section 3: Small Belgian Dogs
  - Section 4: Hairless Dogs
  - Section 5: Tibetan breeds
  - Section 6: Chihuahueño
  - Section 7: English Toy Spaniels
  - Section 8: Japan Chin and Pekingese
  - Section 9: Continental Toy Spaniel
  - Section 10: Kromfohrländer
  - Section 11: Small Molossian type Dogs

- **Group 10 Sighthounds**

  - Section 1: Long-haired or fringed Sighthounds
  - Section 2: Rough-haired Sighthounds
  - Section 3: Short-haired Sighthounds

The Kennel Club

The Kennel Club (UK) is the original and oldest kennel club; it is not a member of the Fédération Cynologique Internationale. For The Kennel Club, dogs are placed in the following groups:

- Hound Group
- Gundog Group
- Terrier Group
- Utility Group
- Working Group

- Pastoral Group
- Toy Group

Working is here meant to indicate dogs that are not hunting dogs that work directly for people, such as police dogs, search and rescue dogs, and others. It does not imply that other types of dogs do not work. Dogs that work with livestock are in the Pastoral Group.

Australia and New Zealand

The Australian National Kennel Council and the New Zealand Kennel Club recognize similar groups to The Kennel Club.

Australian National Kennel Council recognized Breed Groups:

- Group 1 (Toys)
- Group 2 (Terriers)
- Group 3 (Gundogs)
- Group 4 (Hounds)
- Group 5 (Working Dogs)
- Group 6 (Utility)
- Group 7 (Non Sporting)

New Zealand Kennel Club recognized Breed Groups:

- Toy Group
- Terrier Group
- Gundogs
- Hound Group
- Working Group
- Utility Group
- Non Sporting Group

North America

The Canadian Kennel Club and the two major kennel clubs in the United States have similar groups, although they may not include the same dogs in the same groupings. Canadian Kennel Club recognized Breed Groups:

- Group 1, Sporting Dogs
- Group 2, Hounds
- Group 3, Working Dogs
- Group 4, Terriers
- Group 5, Toys
- Group 6, Non-Sporting
- Group 7, Herding

American Kennel Club recognized Breed Groups:

- Sporting Group
- Hound Group
- Working Group
- Terrier Group
- Toy Group
- Non-Sporting Group
- Herding Group

United Kennel Club (US) recognized Breed Groups:

- Companion Dog Group
- Guardian Dog Group
- Gun Dog Group
- Herding Dog Group
- Northern Breed Group
- Scenthound Group
- Sighthound & Pariah Group
- Terrier Group

Other

The major national kennel club for each country will organize breeds in breed groups. The naming and organization of *Breed Groups* may vary from country to country. In addition, some rare new breeds or newly documented traditional breeds may be awaiting approval by a given kennel club, and may not yet be assigned to a particular *Breed Group*.

In addition to the major registries, there are a nearly infinite number of sporting clubs, breed clubs, minor kennel clubs, and internet-based breed registries and dog registration businesses in which breeds may be organized into whatever Breed Group the club, minor registry, or dog business may devise.

See also

- Dog type
- Dog breed
- Conformation show
- General Specials

External links

- http://www.dogsonline.com
- http://www.dogsindepth.com/index.html Dog Breed Groups from dogsindepth.com the online dog encyclopedia
- http://www.u-c-i.de/

American Kennel Club

The **American Kennel Club** (or **AKC**) is a registry of purebred dog pedigrees in the United States. Beyond maintaining its pedigree registry, this kennel club also promotes and sanctions events for purebred dogs, including the Westminster Kennel Club Dog Show, an annual event which predates the official forming of the AKC, the National Dog Show, and the AKC/Eukanuba National Championship. Unlike most other country's kennels clubs, the AKC is not part of the Fédération Cynologique Internationale (World Canine Organization).

Dog registration

The AKC is not the only registry of purebred dogs, but it is the only non-profit registry and the one with which most Americans are familiar. Founded in 1884, the AKC is the largest purebred dog registry in the world. Along with its nearly 5,000 licensed and member clubs and affiliated organizations, the AKC advocates for the purebred dog as a family companion, advances canine health and well-being, works to protect the rights of all dog owners and promotes responsible dog ownership. An example of dogs registered elsewhere in the U.S. is the National Greyhound Association which registers racing greyhounds (which are legally not considered "pets").

For a purebred dog to be registered with the AKC, the dog's parents must be registered with the AKC as the same breed, and the litter in which the dog is born must be registered with the AKC. If the dog's parents are not registered with the AKC or the litter is not registered, special registry research by the AKC is necessary for the AKC to determine if the dog is eligible for AKC registration. Once a determination of eligibility is met, either by litter application or registry research, the dog can be registered as purebred by the AKC.To register a mixed breed dog with AKC as a Canine Partner, you may go to the AKC website and enroll the dog via an online form. Once registered, your mixed breed dog will be eligible to compete in the AKC Agility, Obedience and AKC Rally® Events. 2010 Most Popular Dogs in the U.S.

1. Labrador Retriever

2. German Shepherd Dog

3. Yorkshire Terrier

4. Golden Retriever

5. Beagle

6. Boxer

7. Bulldog

8. Dachshund

9. Poodle

10. Shih Tzu

Registration indicates only that the dog's parents were registered as one recognized breed; it does not necessarily indicate that the dog comes from healthy or show-quality blood lines. Nor is registration necessarily a reflection on the quality of the breeder or how the puppy was raised. Registration is necessary only for breeders (so they can sell registered puppies) or for purebred conformation show or purebred dog sports participation. Registration can be obtained by mail or online at their website.

AKC and health

Even though the AKC supports some canine health research and has run advertising campaigns implying that the AKC is committed to healthy dogs, the AKC's role in furthering dog health is controversial. Temple Grandin maintains that the AKC's standards only regulate physical appearance, not emotional or behavioral health. The AKC has no health standards for breeding. The only breeding restriction is age (a dog can be no younger than 8 months.) Furthermore, the AKC prohibits clubs from imposing stricter regulations, that is, an AKC breed club cannot require a higher breeding age, hip dysplasia ratings, genetic tests for inheritable diseases, or any other restrictions. Parent clubs do have the power to define the looks of the breed, or breed standard. Parent club may also restrict participation in non-regular events or classes such as Futurities or Maturities to only those dogs meeting their defined criteria. This enables those non-regular events to require health testing, DNA sampling, instinct/ability testing and other outlined requirements as established by the hosting club of the non-regular event.

As a result, attention to health among breeders is purely voluntary. By contrast, many dog clubs outside the US do require health tests of breeding dogs. The German Shepherd Club of Germany [1], for example, requires hip and elbow X-rays in addition to other tests before a dog can be bred. Such breeding restrictions are not allowed in AKC member clubs. As a result, some US breeders have established parallel registries or health databases outside of the AKC; for example, the Berner Garde [2] established such a database in 1995 after genetic diseases reduced the average lifespan of a Bernese Mountain Dog to 7 years. The Swiss Bernese Mountain Dog club introduced mandatory hip X-rays in 1971.

For these, and other reasons, a small number of breed clubs have not yet joined the AKC so they can maintain stringent health standards, but, in general, the breeders' desire to show their dogs at AKC shows such as the Westminster Dog Show has won out over these concerns.

Contrary to most western nations organized under the International Kennel Federation (of which the AKC is not a member), the AKC has not removed docked tails and cropped ears from the requirements of many AKC breed standards, even though this practice is opposed in the U.S. by the American Veterinary Medical Association, and banned by law in many other countries.

The Club has also been criticized for courting large scale commercial breeders.

Purebred Alternative Listing Program / Indefinite Listing Privilege Program

The Purebred Alternative Listing Program (PAL), formerly the Indefinite Listing Privilege Program (ILP), is an AKC program that provides purebred dogs who may not have been eligible for registration a chance to register "alternatively" (formerly "indefinitely"). There are various reasons why a purebred dog might not be eligible for registration; for example, the dog may be the product of an unregisterable litter, or have unregisterable parents. Many dogs enrolled in the PAL and ILP programs were adopted from animal shelters or rescue groups, in which case the status of the dog's parents is unknown. Dogs enrolled in PAL/ILP may participate in AKC companion and performance activities, but not conformation. Enrollees of the program receive various benefits, including a subscription to *Family Dog* Magazine, a certificate for their dog's place in the PAL, and information about AKC Pet Healthcare and microchipping. Dogs that were registered under the ILP program keep their original numbers.

AKC National Championship

The AKC/Eukanuba National Championship is an annual event held in both Tampa, FL, and Long Beach, CA. The show is by invitation only. The dogs invited to the show have either finished their championship from the bred-by-exhibitor class or ranked in the Top 25 of their breed. The show can often be seen on major television stations.

Open foundation stock

The Foundation Stock Service (FSS) is an AKC program for breeds not yet accepted by the AKC for full recognition, and not yet in the AKC's Miscellaneous class. The AKC FSS requires that at least the parents of the registered animal are known. The AKC will not grant championship points to dogs in these breeds until the stud book is closed and the breed is granted full recognition.

Activities

The AKC sanctions events in which dogs and handlers can compete. These are divided into three areas:

- Conformation shows
  - Junior Showmanship
- Companion events, in which all registered and PAL/ILP dogs can compete. These include:
  - Obedience trials
  - Tracking trials
  - Dog agility
  - Rally obedience
- Performance events, which are limited to certain entrants; PAL/ILP dogs of the correct breed are usually eligible:
  - Coonhound events (coonhounds; no PAL/ILP dogs)
  - Field trials (hounds)
  - Earthdog trials (small terriers and Dachshunds)
  - Sheepdog trials (herding tests) (herding breeds, Rottweilers, and Samoyeds)
  - Hunt tests (most dogs in the Sporting Groups and Standard Poodles)
  - Lure coursing (sighthounds only)
  - Working Dog Sport (obedience, tracking, protection) German Shepherds, Doberman Pinschers, Rottweilers, Bouvier des Flandres

AKC policy toward working dog sport events that include protection phases, such as Schutzhund, has changed according to prevailing public sentiment in the United States. In 1990, as well-publicized dog attacks were driving public fear against many breeds, the AKC issued a ban on protection sports for all of its member clubs. After the terrorist attacks of 9/11/2001, Americans began to take a more positive attitude toward well-trained protection dogs, and in July 2003 the AKC decided to allow member clubs to hold a limited number of protection events with prior written permission. In 2006 the AKC released rules for its own Working Dog Sport events, very similar to Schutzhund.

In 2007, the American Kennel Club accepted an invitation from the Mexican Kennel Club to participate in the Fédération Cynologique Internationale World Dog Show in Mexico City.

Recognized breeds

As of July 2009, the AKC fully recognizes 163 breeds with 12 additional breeds granted partial status in the Miscellaneous class. Another 62 rare breeds can be registered in its Foundation Stock Service.

The AKC divides dog breeds into seven *groups*, one *class*, and the Foundation Stock Service, consisting of the following (as of July 2009):

- Sporting Group: 28 breeds developed as bird dogs. Includes Pointers, Retrievers, Setters, and Spaniels.
- Hound Group: 25 breeds developed to hunt using sight (sighthounds) or scent (scent hounds). Includes Greyhounds and Beagles.
- Working Group: 26 large breeds developed for a variety of jobs, including guarding property, guarding livestock, or pulling carts. Includes Siberian Huskies and Bernese Mountain Dogs.
- Terrier Group: 27 feisty breeds some of which were developed to hunt vermin and to dig them from their burrows or lairs. Size ranges from the tiny Cairn Terrier to the large Airedale Terrier.
- Toy Group: 21 small companion breeds Includes Toy Poodles and Pekineses.
- Non-Sporting Group: 17 breeds that do not fit into any of the preceding categories, usually larger than Toy dogs. Includes Bichon Frises and Miniature Poodles.
- Herding Group: 22 breeds developed to herd livestock. Includes Rough Collies and Belgian Shepherds.
- Best in Show:over 150 breeds All Breeds
- Miscellaneous Class: 11 breeds that have advanced from FSS but that are not yet fully recognized. After a period of time that ensures that good breeding practices are in effect and that the gene pool for the breed is ample, the breed is moved to one of the seven preceding groups.
- Foundation Stock Service (FSS) Program: 62 breeds. This is a breed registry in which breeders of rare breeds can record the birth and parentage of a breed that they are trying to establish in the United States; these dogs provide the *foundation stock* from which eventually a fully recognized breed might result. These breeds cannot participate in AKC events until at least 150 individual dogs are registered; thereafter, competition in various events is then provisional.

The AKC Board of Directors appointed a committee in October, 2007, to evaluate the current alignment of breeds within the seven variety groups. Reasons for the action included the growing number of breeds in certain groups, and the make-up of breeds within certain groups. The number of groups and group make-up has been modified in the past, providing precedent for this action. The Group Realignment Committee completed their report in July, 2008.

The committee recommended that the seven variety groups be replaced with ten variety groups. If this proposal is approved, the Hound Group would be divided into "Scent Hounds" and "Sight Hounds"; the Sporting Group would be divided into "Sporting Group – Pointers and Setters" and "Sporting Group –

Retrievers and Spaniels"; a new group called the "Northern Group" would be created; and the Non-Sporting Group would be renamed the "Companion Group". The Northern Group would be populated by Northern/Spitz breeds, consisting of the Norwegian Elkhound, Akita, Alaskan Malamute, Siberian Husky, Samoyed, American Eskimo, Chinese Shar-Pei, Chow Chow, Finnish Spitz, Keeshond, Schipperke, Shiba Inu and Swedish Vallhund. In addition, the Italian Greyhound is proposed to be moved to the Sight Hound Group, and the Dalmatian is proposed to be moved to the Working Group.

See also: American Kennel Club Groups

Other AKC programs

The AKC also offers the Canine Good Citizen program. This program tests dogs of any breed (including mixed breed) or type, registered or not, for basic behavior and temperament suitable for appearing in public and living at home.

The AKC also supports Canine Health with the Canine Health Foundation http://www.akcchf.org/

Another AKC affiliate is AKC Companion Animal Recovery (AKC CAR), the nation's largest not-for-profit pet identification and 24/7 recovery service provider. AKC CAR is a leading distributor of pet microchips in the U.S. and a participant in AAHA's free Pet Microchip Lookup tool.

AKC and legislation

The AKC tracks all dog related legislation in the United States, lobbies lawmakers and issues legislative alerts on the internet asking for citizens to contact public officials. They are particularly active in combating breed-specific legislation such as bans on certain breeds considered dangerous. They also combat most legislation to protect animals such as breed-limit restrictions and anti-puppy mill legislation. While they argue that their motive is to protect legitimate breeders and the industry, many argue their incentive is purely financial.

See also

- List of dog breeds
- United Kennel Club
- DOGNY
- American Dog Club
- World Wide Kennel Club
- List of Kennel Clubs by Country

External links

- Official website [3]
- AKC CAR's Official website [4]
- 2007 Registration Data [5]
- The Politics of Dogs: Criticism of Policies of AKC [6] The Atlantic, 1990
- Digging into the AKC: Taking cash for tainted dogs [7] The Philadelphia Inquirer, 1995
- Doogle.Info Worldwide online dog database and pedigree [8]

Non-Sporting Group

The **Non-Sporting Group** of dogs is a kennel club dog breed Group designation. How *Non-Sporting* is defined varies among kennel clubs, and different kennel clubs may not include the same breeds in their *Non-Sporting Group*. Some kennel clubs do not use the *Non-Sporting* classification. *Non-Sporting Group* is not a term used by the international kennel club association, the Fédération Cynologique Internationale, which more finely divides its breed groupings by dog type and breed history.

For the American Kennel Club and the Canadian Kennel Club, the *Non-Sporting Group* is a diverse classification. Here are sturdy animals with as different personalities and appearances as the Chow Chow, and Keeshond. The breeds in the *Non-Sporting Group* are a varied collection in terms of size, coat, personality and overall appearance.

Non-Sporting Group breeds

American Kennel Club

American Eskimo Dog	Bichon Frise	Boston Terrier
Bulldog	Chinese Shar-Pei	Chow Chow
Dalmatian	Finnish Spitz	French Bulldog
Keeshond	Lhasa Apso	Löwchen
Poodle	Schipperke	Shiba Inu
Tibetan Spaniel	Tibetan Terrier	

Canadian Kennel Club

The Canadian Kennel Club recognizes most of the same breeds as the American Kennel Club as Non-Sporting, with a few exceptions.

Mexican Hairless Dog

American Eskimo Dog

The American Eskimo is a small to medium-size Nordic-type dog, which looks like a miniature Samoyed. There are three varieties: the toy, miniature, and standard. The American Eskimo has a wedge-shaped head with muzzle and skull about the same length. It has erect triangular-shaped ears, and a heavily plumed tail curled over the back. The coat is always white, or white with biscuit or cream markings. Their skin is pink or gray. The coat is heavy around the neck, creating a ruff or mane, especially in males. The breed is slightly longer than it is tall. It is sometimes mistaken for the Japanese Spitz and the Samoyed Dog.

History

The American Eskimo Dog ("Eskie") "is a modern variation of a very ancient family of dogs." Spitz type dogs developed in Arctic and northern areas of the world, with the larger types being used as sled dogs. American Eskimo Dogs are used to climates either in the negatives and can withstand the heat but rather the snow. These dogs resemble wolves and absolutelly adore rain, snow or shine. They will do well in any climate area but not recomended for warmer climates all year round.\ But the Eskie was specifically bred to guard people and property and, therefore, is territorial by nature and an excellent watch dog. He is very loyal to his family and is known for being gentle and playful with children. He is energetic, alert and highly intelligent. In Northern Europe, smaller Spitz were kept primarily as pets and watchdogs, and eventually were developed into the various German Spitz breeds. European immigrants brought their Spitz pets with them to the United States, especially New York, in the early 1900s, "all of them descended from the larger German Spitz, the Keeshond, the white Pomeranian, and the Italian Spitz, the Volpino Italiano."

Although white was not always a recognized color in the various German Spitz breeds, it was generally the preferred color in the US. In a display of patriotism in the era around World War I, dog owners began referring to their pets as American Spitz rather than German Spitz. This name change was similar to the use in the United States of the term Freedom fries rather than French fries to refer to a popular potato dish during disputes between France and the United States before the 2003 invasion of Iraq.

After World War I, the small Spitz dogs came to the attention of the American public when the dogs became popular entertainers in the American circus. In 1917, the Cooper Brother's Railroad Circus featured the dogs. A dog named Stout's Pal Pierre was famous for walking a tightrope with the Barnum and Bailey Circus in the 1930s. Due to the popularity of the circus dogs, many of today's American Eskimo Dogs can trace their lineage back to these circus dogs.

After World War II, the dogs continued to be popular pets. Postwar contact with Japan led to importation into the United States of the Japanese Spitz, which may have been crossed into the breed at this time. The breed was first officially recognized as the "American Eskimo" as early as 1919 by the American United Kennel Club (UKC), and the first written record and history of the breed was printed in 1958 by the UKC. At that time there was no official breed club and no breed standard, and dogs were accepted for registration as single dogs, based on appearance. In 1970 the National American Eskimo Dog Association (NAEDA) was founded, and single dog registrations ceased. In 1985 the American Eskimo Dog Club of America (AEDCA) was formed by fanciers who wished to register the breed with the American Kennel Club (AKC). Following the AKC's requirements for breed recognition, the AEDCA collected the pedigree information from 1,750 dogs that now form the basis of the AKC recognized breed, which is called the American Eskimo Dog. The breed was recognized by the American Kennel Club in 1995. The stud book was opened from 2000 to 2003 in an attempt to register more of the original UKC registered lines, and today many American Eskimo Dogs are dual-registered with both American kennel clubs. The breed is also recognized by the Canadian Kennel Club as of 2006, but is not recognized elsewhere in the world.

The American Eskimo Dog is not an internationally recognized breed, and since neither of the American kennel clubs are affiliated with the Fédération Cynologique Internationale, fanciers wishing to participate in international dog shows will register their American Eskimo Dogs as the very similar German Spitz. This is done only by individuals wishing to participate in dog sports in international shows, and does not mean that the American Eskimo Dog and the German Spitz are the same. The breeds may have the same general origins, but have developed differently over the past 100 years.

Health

Health testing should be performed by all responsible breeders and anyone purchasing a puppy should be aware of the genetic problems which have been found in some individuals of the breed, such as PRA (Progressive Retinal Atrophy), luxating patella, and hip dysplasia. None of these are common and the breed is generally healthy.

In addition to the problems above, the breed can have a tendency towards allergies and tear-staining, and the propensity towards these traits is inherited.

Temperament

American Eskimos can be prone to 'fear biting', they are generally wary of strangers and often bite if a person attempts to pet them without getting to know them first. They are very lovable and sweet to their owner and would not likely bite a family member. Eskimos would not be a wise choice for a family with small children and would do better for an older couple or a family with children over thirteen years of age. American Eskimo Dogs, along with other Spitz, were bred to be house dogs and companion dogs and thrive on being a part of a human family. The Eskie is highly intelligent, eager to please, very active, has lots of energy, and moderately independent. At home, these lively dogs make excellent watchdogs, barking to announce the presence of strangers. The Eskie can be protective of its home and family, but in general, they will not threaten to attack or bite a person unless provoked. As with all dogs, behavior is partially inherited and partially trained. Some dogs are prone to excessive barking and separation anxiety. It is important for puppy buyers to research pedigrees as temperament may vary due to inheritance.

Grooming and training

Eskie's double coat needs brushing and combing twice weekly, more often when their biannual shedding occurs. An undercoat rake, a tool available at most pet stores, is useful for brushing out the heavy undercoat. Some owners in hot climates do shave their Eskies, but if this is done, the dogs should be kept indoors as much as possible to prevent sunburn. The breed's shedding, along with its active temperament, results in some dogs being taken to animal shelters or otherwise put up for adoption. Owners should contact breed-specific rescue groups that will give advice on grooming, training or curbing behavioral issues.

American Eskimo Dogs are very energetic and require daily exercise, the extent of the workout depending on the size of the dog. Owners can avoid problems by socializing their Eskie through obedience training or participating in dog sports, such as dog agility, flyball, and dancing.

See also

- Breed club (dog)
- German Spitz
- Northern Breed Group
- Spitz

Bichon Frise

A **Bichon Frisé** (French, meaning *curly white lap dog*) is a small breed of dog of the Bichon type. They are popular pets, similar in appearance to, but larger than, the Maltese. They are a non-shedding breed that requires daily grooming. This lack of shedding makes the Bichon Frisé a very good dog for people who have allergies.

History

The Bichon Frisé descended from the Barbet or Water Spaniel, from which came the name "Barbichon", later shortened to "Bichon". The Bichons were divided into four categories: the Bichon Malteise, the Bichon Bolognaise, the Bichon Havanese and the Bichon Tenerife. All originated in the Mediterranean area.

Because of their merry disposition, they traveled much and were often used as barter by sailors as they moved from continent to continent. The dogs found early success in Spain and it is generally believed that Spanish seamen introduced the breed to the Canary Island of Tenerife. In the 1300s, Italian sailors rediscovered the little dogs on their voyages and are credited with returning them to the continent, where they became great favorites of Italian nobility. Often, as was the style of the day with dogs in the courts, they were cut "lion style," like a modern-day Portuguese Water Dog.

Though not considered a retriever or water dog, the Bichon, due to its ancestry as a sailor's dog, has an affinity for and enjoys water and retrieving. On the boats however, the dog's job was that of a companion dog.

The "Tenerife", or "Bichon", had success in France during the Renaissance under Francis I (1515–47), but its popularity skyrocketed in the court of Henry III (1574–89). The breed also enjoyed considerable success in Spain as a favorite of the Infantas, and painters of the Spanish school often included them in their works. For example, the famous artist, Francisco de Goya, included a Bichon in several of his works.

Interest in the breed was renewed during the rule of Napoleon III, but then waned until the late 1800s when it became the "common dog", running the streets, accompanying the organ grinders of Barbary, leading the blind and doing tricks in circuses and fairs.

On 5 March 1933, the official standard of the breed was adopted by the Société Centrale Canine, the national kennel club for France. (This was largely due to the success of the French-speaking Belgian author Hergé's "Tintin" books, which featured a small, fluffy, white dog named Milou.) As the breed was known by two names at that time, "Tenerife" and "Bichon", the president of the Fédération Cynologique Internationale proposed a name based on the characteristics that the dogs presented - the Bichon Frisé. ("Frisé" means "curly", referring to the breed's coat.) On 18 October 1934, the Bichon

Frisé was admitted to the stud book of the Société Centrale Canine.

The Bichon was popularised in Australia in the mid 1960s, largely thanks to the Channel Nine mini-series Meweth, starring Bruce Gyngell alongside his pet Bichon, Molly. The show ran for one season only, however it gained a cult following. In subsequent years Bichon ownership, especially in the Eastern states, climbed dramatically.

The Bichon was brought to the United States in 1955, and was recognized by the American Kennel Club in 1973. The first US-born Bichon litter was whelped in 1956. In 1959 and 1960, two breeders in different parts of the USA acquired Bichons, which provided the origins for the breed's development in the USA.

The Bichon Frisé became eligible to enter the AKC's Miscellaneous Class on 1 September 1971. In October, 1972, the breed was admitted to registration in the American Kennel Club Stud Book. On 4 April 1973, the breed became eligible to show in the Non-Sporting Group at AKC dog shows.

Description

Appearance

The Bichon Frisé is a small dog that weighs approximately 5 − 10 kg (10 - 20 lbs) and stands 23 − 30 cm (9 − 12 in) at the withers, but slightly larger dogs are not uncommon. It has a black nose and dark round eyes, and its white hair consists of a curly outercoat and a silky undercoat, although many of the breed do tend to have less curly hair than others. As the hair of these dogs gets matted it may become a sort of orangeish colour. A small amount of buff, cream, or apricot colour may be seen around its ears, snout, paws or body, but normally these colours do not exceed 10% of its body. The head and legs are proportionate in size to the body, and the ears and tail are natural (not *docked* or *cropped*). The coat is trimmed often to make the hair seem like an even length. Bichon Frises can be medium-high intelligence.

Temperament

The AKC refers to the Bichon Frisé as "merry" and "cheerful", and the breed standard calls for a dog that is "gentle mannered, sensitive, playful and affectionate". Bred to be companion dogs, the Bichon Frisé tends to get along well with both children and other animals.

Bichon Frisés are very obedient if training is started early and continued consistently.

Hypoallergenic qualities and shedding

Bichon Frisés often appear on lists of dogs that do not shed (moult), but this is misleading. The grooming required to maintain the Bichon Frisé's coat helps remove loose hair, and the curl in the coat helps prevent dead hair and dander from escaping into the environment, as with the poodle's coat. The frequent trimming, brushing, and bathing required to keep the Bichon looking its best removes hair and dander and controls the other potent allergen, saliva.

Bichon Frisés are considered suitable for people with allergies , as they are bred to be hypoallergenic. However, it is important to note that, human sensitivity to dog fur, dander, and saliva varies considerably. Although hair, dander, and saliva can be minimised, they are still present and can stick to "clothes and the carpets and furnishings in your home"; inhaling the allergens, or being licked by the dog, can trigger a reaction in a sensitive person.

Mortality (Longevity)

Bichon Frisé in (combined)UK and USA/Canada surveys had an average life span of about 15 years, with Bichon Frisés in the UK tending to live longer than Bichon Frises in the USA/Canada. This breed's longevity is similar to other breeds of its size and a little longer than for purebred dogs in general. The longest lived of 34 deceased Bichons in a 2004 UK survey died at 16.5 years.

The oldest Bichon Frisés for which there are reliable records in various USA/Canada surveys have died at 19 years.

In a 2004 UK Kennel Club survey, the leading causes of Bichon Frise death were old age (23.5%) and cancer (21%). In a 2007 USA/Canada breeders survey, the leading causes of death were cancer (22%), unknown causes (14%), haematologic (11%), and old age (10%). Haematologic causes of death were divided between autoimmune haemolytic anemia (AIHA) and immune-mediated thrombocytopenia (ITP). AIHA and ITP were responsible for the greatest amount of Bichon Frisé "years lost." "Years lost" is a measure of the extent to which a condition kills members of a breed prematurely. While cancer is a more common cause of death than AIHA/ITP, Bichon Frisés that died of cancer died at a median age of 12.5 years. Haematologic deaths occurred at a median age of only 5 years. Bichon Frisés in the UK survey had a lower rate of haematologic deaths (3%) than in the USA/Canada survey (11%).

Bichons are also prone to liver shunts. These often go undetected until later in life, leading to complications that cannot be fixed, and therefore liver failure. Bichons who are underweight, the runts of the litter, or have negative reactions to food high in protein are likely to be suffering from a shunt. When detected early, shunt often can be corrected through surgery. However, the later in life the shunt is detected, the lower the likelihood of surgery being a success becomes. Shunts can be kept under control through special diets of low protein. (Hill's Prescription diet K/D or L/D), and through various medications to support liver function, help flush toxins that build up in the kidneys and liver, and control seizures that often occur as a symptom of the shunt. Without surgery, Bichons with shunts on average live to be 4–6 years old. If you own a smaller than average size bichon please consult your vet. Other symptoms include dark urine, lethargy, loss of appetite, increase in drinking. Also seizures come in all forms; episodes of seizures can begin early on but go undetected. Early seizures can appear to be seeing the bichon in a hypnotic state (staring at something not there), or to be experiencing an episode of vertigo, or being drunk. Shunts are a serious condition of smaller breeds, and often not associated with Bichons. But more and more bichons are being afflicted by this condition.

AIHA and ITP

Because autoimmune haemolytic anaemia (AIHA, also called immune-mediated haemolytic anemia, or IMHA) and immune-mediated thrombocytopenia (ITP) are responsible for premature Bichon Frisé deaths, Bichon Frisé owners should be particularly alert to the symptoms of these conditions. In AIHA, the dog's immune system attacks its own red blood cells, leading to severe, life-threatening anaemia. Symptoms include weakness, loss of energy, lack of appetite, vomiting, diarrhoea, rapid heart rate, rapid breathing, dark urine, and pale or yellow gums. Thrombocytopenia often accompanies AIHA. In ITP, blood platelets (which cause blood clotting) are destroyed. The most common clinical signs are haemorrhages of the skin and mucus membranes. Owners of Bichon Frisés showing suspicious symptoms should seek immediate veterinary care as these diseases can strike with little or no warning and kill very quickly. Mortality rates of 20% to 80% are reported.

See also

- Companion Dog Group
- Companion dog
- Toy Group
- Non-Sporting Group

Boston Terrier

The **Boston Terrier** is a breed of dog originating in the United States of America. This "American Gentleman" was accepted in 1893 by the American Kennel Club as a non-sporting breed. Color and markings are important when distinguishing this breed to the AKC standard. They should be either black, brindle or seal with white markings. Bostons are small and compact with a short tail and erect ears. They are intelligent and friendly and can be stubborn at times. The average life span of a Boston is 13 years.

History

The Boston Terrier breed originated around 1870, when Robert C. Hooper of Boston purchased a dog known as Hooper's Judge, who was of a Bull and Terrier type lineage. Judge's specific lineage is unknown, however, Hooper's Judge is either directly related to the original Bull and Terrier breeds of the 1700s and early 1800s, or Judge is the result of modern English Bulldogs being crossed into terriers created in the 1860s for show purposes, like the White English Terrier.

Judge weighed over 29.7 pounds (13.5 kilos). Their offspring interbred with one or more French Bulldogs, providing the foundation for the Boston Terrier. Bred down in size from pit-fighting dogs of the Bull and Terrier types, the Boston Terrier originally weighed up to 44 pounds (20 kg.) (Olde Boston Bulldogge). The breed was first shown in Boston in 1870. By 1889 the breed had become sufficiently popular in Boston that fanciers formed the American Bull Terrier Club, but this proposed name for the breed was not well received by the Bull Terrier Fanciers; the breed's nickname, "roundheads", was similarly inappropriate. Shortly after, at the suggestion of James Watson (a noted writer and authority), the club changed its name to the Boston Terrier Club and in 1893 it was admitted to membership in the American Kennel Club, thus making it the first US breed to be recognized. It is one of a small number of breeds to have originated in the United States. The Boston Terrier was the first non-sporting dog bred in the US.

In the early years, the color and markings were not very important, but by the 1900s the breed's distinctive markings and color were written into the standard, becoming an essential feature. Terrier only in name, the Boston Terrier has lost most of its ruthless desire for mayhem, preferring the company of humans, although some males will still challenge other dogs if they feel their territory is being invaded.

Boston Terriers were particularly popular during the 1920s in the US.

Description

Appearance

The Boston Terrier is a lively and highly intelligent breed. Typical physical traits include a smooth coat, and both a short head and tail resulting in a balanced compact build. Coloring is primarily brindle, seal or black in color and evenly marked with white. The head is in proportion to the size of the dog and the expression indicates a high degree of intelligence.

The body is rather short and well knit, the limbs strong and neatly turned, the tail is short and no feature is so prominent that the dog appears badly proportioned. The dog conveys an impression of determination, strength and activity, with style of a high order; carriage easy and graceful. A proportionate combination of "Color and White Markings" is a particularly distinctive feature of a representative specimen.

"Balance, Expression, Color and White Markings" should be given particular consideration in determining the relative value of *general appearance* to other points.

Size

Boston Terriers are typically small, compactly built, well proportioned dogs with erect ears, short tails, and a short muzzle that should be free of wrinkles. They usually have a square sort of face. According to international breed standard, the dog should weigh no less than 10 pounds and no more than 25 pounds. Boston Terriers usually stand 15-17 inches at the withers.

Coat and color

The Boston Terrier is characteristically marked with white in proportion to either black, brindle, seal, or a combination of the three. Seal is a color specifically used to describe Boston Terriers and is defined as a black color with red highlights when viewed in the sun or bright light. Black, Brindle, and Seal (all on white) are the only colors recognized by the AKC. There are also liver, brown, cream or red and white Boston Terriers, however these marking are more rare than the others listed above, and are disqualified from AKC events. If all other qualities are identical, brindle is the preferred color according to most breed standards.

Ideally, white should cover its chest, muzzle, band around the neck, half way up the forelegs, up to the hocks on the rear legs, and a white blaze between but not touching the eyes. For conformation showing, symmetrical markings are preferred. Due to the Boston Terrier's markings resembling formal wear, in addition to its refined and pleasant personality, the breed is commonly referred to as the "American Gentleman."

Temperament

Boston Terriers have strong, friendly personalities. Bostons can range in temperaments from those that are eager to please their master to those that are more stubborn. Both can be easily trained given a patient and assertive owner.

While originally bred for fighting, they were later down bred for companionship. The modern Boston Terrier can be gentle, alert, expressive, and well-mannered. It must be noted however, that they are not considered terriers by the American Kennel Club, but are part of the non-sporting group. Boston Terrier is something of a misnomer. They were originally a cross-breed between the Old English Bulldog and the English White Terrier.

Some Bostons enjoy having another one for companionship. Both females and males generally bark only when necessary. Having been bred as a companion dog, they enjoy being around people, and, if properly socialized, get along well with children, the elderly, other canines, and non-canine pets. Some Boston Terriers are very cuddly, while others are more independent.

Health

Several health issues are of concern in the Boston Terrier: cataracts (both juvenile and adult type), cherry eye, luxating patellas, deafness, heart murmur, and allergies. Curvature of the back, called roaching, might be caused by patella problems with the rear legs, which in turn causes the dog to lean forward onto the forelegs. This might also just be a structural fault with little consequence to the dog. Many Bostons cannot tolerate excessive heat and also extremely cold weather, due to the shortened muzzle, so hot or cold weather combined with demanding exercise can bring harm to a Boston Terrier. A sensitive digestive system is also typical of the Boston Terrier. In the absence of proper diet, flatulence is associated with the breed. Boston Terriers take in air while they eat and this causes high flatulence.

Bostons, along with Pug, Shih Tzu and other short-snouted breeds are brachycephalic breeds. The word comes from Greek roots "Brachy," meaning short and "cephalic," meaning head. This anatomy can cause tiny nostrils, long palates and a narrow trachea. Because of this, Bostons may be prone to snoring and reverse sneeze, a rapid and repeated forced inhalation through the nose, accompanied by snorting or gagging sounds used to clear the palate of mucus, but does not harm the dog in any way.

See also

- Companion dog
- Companion Dog Group
- Non-Sporting Group

References

Further reading

- Bulanda, Susan (1994). *Boston Terriers*. Barron's Educational Series, Inc. ISBN 0-8120-1696-3.

External links

- Boston Terrier Club of America, Inc. [1]
- Boston Terrier Club of Canada [2]
- (First published 1910)
- An article on Helium about the Boston Terrier [3]

Bulldog

A **Bulldog** is the common name for a breed of dog also referred to as the **English Bulldog** or **British Bulldog**. Other bulldog breeds include the American Bulldog and the French Bulldog. The Bulldog is a muscular heavy dog with a wrinkled face and a distinctive pushed-in nose. The American Kennel Club (AKC), The Kennel Club (UK) and the United Kennel Club (UKC) oversee breeding standards.

Description

Appearance

The bulldog is a breed with characteristically thick shoulders and a matching head. There are generally thick folds of skin on a bulldog's brow, followed by round, black, wide-set eyes, a short muzzle with characteristic folds called "rope" above the nose, with hanging skin under the neck, drooping lips, and pointed teeth. The coat is short, flat and sleek, with colors of red, fawn, white, brindle (mixed colors, often in waves or irregular stripes), and piebalds of these.

In the US, the size of a typical mature male is about 45 pounds and that for mature females is about 45 pounds for a Standard English Bulldog. In the United Kingdom, the breed standard is 55 pounds for a male and 50 pounds for a female.

While some canine breeds require their tails to be cut or docked soon after birth, bulldogs are one of very few breeds whose tail is naturally short and curled. A longer upright tail is a serious fault in a show bulldog.

Temperament

Despite their famous "sourpuss" expression, bulldogs are generally docile although can prove to be very fast movers over a short distance. They are friendly and gregarious but occasionally willful. The phrase "stubborn as a bulldog" is loosely rooted in fact. They rank 77th out of 79 in Stanley Coren's The Intelligence of Dogs, being of lowest degree working/obedience intelligence.

Breeders have worked to breed aggression out of the breed, and as such the dog is known to be of generally good temperament. Bulldogs can be so attached to home and family that they will not venture out of the yard without a human companion. Due to their friendly nature bulldogs are known for getting along well with children, other dogs and pets.

Health

Statistics from the Orthopedic Foundation for Animals indicate that of the 467 Bulldogs tested, 73.9% were affected by hip dysplasia, the highest amongst all breeds. Similarly, the breed has the worst score in the British Veterinary Association/Kennel Club Hip Dysplasia scoring scheme, although only 22 Bulldogs were tested in the Scheme. Patellar luxation is another condition which affects 6.2% of Bulldogs .

Some individuals of this breed are prone to interdigital cysts, which are cysts that form between the toes. These cause the dog some discomfort, but are treatable either by vet or an experienced owner. They may also suffer from respiratory problems.

Other problems can include cherry eye, a protrusion of the inner eyelid (which can be corrected by a veterinarian), certain allergies, and hip issues in older bulldogs. Puppies are frequently delivered by Caesarean section because their characteristically large heads can become lodged in the mother's birth canal during natural birth. However, it is not entirely uncommon for a bulldog to whelp naturally and successfully. Over 80% of Bulldog litters are delivered by Caesarean section. The folds or "rope" on a Bulldogs face should be cleaned daily to avoid unwanted infections caused by moisture accumulation. Also, some bulldogs' naturally curling tails can be so tight to the body as to require regular cleaning and a bit of ointment.

Like all dogs, bulldogs require daily exercise. If not properly exercised it is possible for a bulldog to become overweight, which could lead to heart and lung problems, as well as joint issues.

Bulldogs are very sensitive to heat. Extra caution should be practiced in warmer climates and during summer months. Bulldogs must be given plenty of shade and water, and **must** be kept out of standing heat. Air conditioning and good ventilation is required to keep them healthy and safe. Bulldogs actually do most of their sweating through the pads on their feet. You will notice bulldogs really enjoy cool floors such as tile or cement. This helps keep them cool. Due to the airway obstruction problem bulldogs may have, like all "short-faced" breeds they can easily get overheated and even die from hyperthermia. They can be big snorters and heavy breathers due to this obstruction and also tend to be loud snorers. These are all issues that are easy to keep under control as long as you stay aware and protect your bulldog from these unsafe conditions.(EngBulldogs.com)

In January 2009, after the BBC documentary *Pedigree Dogs Exposed*, the The Kennel Club introduced revised breed standards for the British Bulldog, along with 209 other breeds, to address health concerns. Opposed by the British Bulldog Breed Council, it was speculated by the press that the changes would lead to a smaller head, less skin folds, a longer muzzle, and a taller thinner posture, in order to combat perceived problems with respiration and with breeding due to head size and width of shoulders.

History

The term "bulldog" was first mentioned in literature around 1500, the oldest spelling of the word being Bondogge and Bolddogge. The first reference to the word with the modern spelling is dated 1631 or 1632 in a letter by a man named Preswick Eaton where he writes: "procuer mee two good Bulldoggs, and let them be sent by ye first shipp". The origins of the Bulldog are vague with some sources suggesting it developed from a cross of three different breeds: the Pug, the Mastiff, and a breed of Spanish dog. The name "bull" was applied because of the dog's use in the sport of bull baiting. The original Bulldog had to be very ferocious and so savage and courageous as to be almost insensitive to pain. In 1835 dog fighting as a sport became illegal in England. Therefore, the Old English Bulldog had outlived his usefulness in England and his days were numbered in England. However, emigrants did have a use for such dogs in the New World, resulting in the original Bulldog's closest descendant, the American Bulldog. Back in England, they proceeded to eliminate the undesirable 'fierce' characteristics and to preserve and accentuate the finer qualities. Within a few generations, the English Bulldog became one of the finest physical specimens, minus its original viciousness, stamina, strength, speed, and intelligence.

It has been theorized that bulldogs were bred in England as a cross between the Mastiff, the Pug, and a breed of Spanish dog, although this genetic origin is debated.

In the 1600s, bulldogs were used for bullbaiting (as well as bearbaiting)—a gambling sport popular in the 17th century with wagers laid while trained bulldogs leapt at a bull lashed to a post. The bulldog's typical means of attack included latching onto the animal's snout and attempting to suffocate it.

However, the bulldog's early role was not limited to sport. In mid-17th century New York, bulldogs were used as a part of a city-wide round-up effort led by governor Richard Nicolls. Because cornering and leading wild bulls was dangerous, bulldogs were trained to seize a bull by its nose long enough for a rope to be secured around its neck.. The use of dogs for fighting with other dogs or other animals was banned in the United Kingdom by the Cruelty to Animals Act 1835, but Bulldogs as pets were continually promoted by dog dealer Bill George.

In time, the original old English bulldog was crossed with the pug. The outcome was a shorter, wider dog with a brachycephalic skull. Though today's bulldog looks tough, he cannot perform the job he was originally created for, as he cannot withstand the rigors of running and being thrown from a bull, and cannot grip with such a short muzzle.

The oldest single breed specialty club is The Bulldog Club (England), which was formed in 1878. Members of this club met frequently at the Blue Post pub on Oxford Street in London. There they wrote the first standard of perfection for the breed. In 1891 the two top bulldogs, Orry and Dockleaf, competed in a contest to see which dog could walk the farthest. Orry was reminiscent of the original bulldogs, lighter boned and very athletic. Dockleaf was smaller and heavier set, more like modern bulldogs. Dockleaf was declared the winner that year. Although some argued that the older version of the bulldog was more fit to perform, the modern version's looks won over the fans of the breed because they proved they were equally as fit and athletic in the walking competition.

At the turn of the 20th century, Ch. Rodney Stone became the first Bulldog to command a price of $5000 when he was bought by controversial Irish-American political figure Richard Croker.

Popular mascot

The British/English Bulldog is one of the four national animals of the United Kingdom. The breed is the official mascot of the United States Marine Corps and many bases have their own mascot on base. Thirty-nine American universities use a bulldog as their mascot. This includes mascots such as Bryant University's Tupper the Bulldog, Yale University's Handsome Dan, Georgetown University's Jack the Bulldog, the University of Georgia's Uga, Gonzaga University's Spike, Butler University's Blue, Louisiana Tech University's Tech, Mississippi State's Bully, Western Illinois University's [1] Rocky [2], the University of North Carolina at Asheville's Rocky [3], Fresno State's Timeout, Drake University's Spike and Omega Psi Phi Fraternity, Inc's Dawg, James Madison University's DUKE DOG.

See also

- Companion dog
- Companion Dog Group
- Molosser
- Non-Sporting Group

Shar Pei

The **Shar Pei**, or **Chinese Shar-Pei**, is a breed of dog known for its distinctive features of deep wrinkles and a blue-black tongue. The breed comes from China. The name (沙皮, pinyin: *shā pí*; English name probably derived from British spelling of the Cantonese equivalent, *sā pèih*) translates to "sand skin" and refers to the texture of its short, rough coat. As puppies, Shar Pei have numerous wrinkles, but as they mature, these wrinkles disappear as they "grow into their skin". Shar Pei were once named as one of the world's rarest dog breeds by *Time* magazine and the *Guinness Book of World Records*, and the American Kennel Club did not recognize the breed until 1991.

History and origin

The origin of the Chinese Shar-Pei can be traced to the province of Guangdong and has existed for centuries in the southern provinces of China. These dogs helped their peasant masters with various tasks, such as herding cattle and guarding the home and family, and have proven themselves to be qualified hunters of wild game—usually wild pigs—and, of course, they were used for generations as fighting dogs by the Chinese nobility, although the practice became rarer after the people's revolution, when such activities were seen as the preserve of the decadent classes.

The Shar-Pei is believed to have shared a common origin with the smooth-coated Chow-Chow because of the blue-black mouths and tongues; possibly the Great Pyrenees, a source of the double dew claws; and the Tibetan Mastiff. It was believed in ancient times that the dark mouth of the Chow-Chow, exposed when barking, helped to ward off evil spirits. Shar-Pei, when translated, means "sand skin" or "shark skin". This uniquely rough, loose, prickly coat enabled the Shar-Pei to wriggle out of its opponent's grasp while fighting in the dog pits. When stroked against the grain, the coat may be abrasive, producing a burning, itching sensation. The tail is carried over the back on either side, exposing the anus. The first tail set is a tightly curled tail, a "coin" tail. The second tail set is the loose curl, and the third is carried in an arch over the back. Any Shar-Pei with its tail sticking out straight or between its legs was thought to be cowardly. The tail should denote bravery.

According to old-time dog-fighting fanciers, when a dog's toes were slightly turned out as the body was viewed head-on, it was thought to help the dog with balance. The Chinese crawling dragon with its feet pointed east and west was considered a sign of strength. Because of poor breeding practices, many of the Shar-Pei have bad fronts. A dog with straight forelegs is correct.

Incidentally, Western breeders maintain that any dog in China that protects property is called a fighting dog, whereas in Canada and the United States, they are referred to as guard dogs. This is still a moot point. Up until the introduction of Breed Specific Legislation, designed to target breeds alleged to be "more likely" to attack and largely aimed at criminalising the American Pit Bull Terrier, the Shar-Pei was regarded as a breed designed, bred and selected for dog fighting. After the introduction of various

Breed Specific Legislation, many breeders started to deny the fighting ancestry and concocted fanciful tales of a hunting heritage. It is worth mentioning that the Chinese and Taiwanese still regard the Shar-Pei as a dog-fighting breed, although the prohibitive cost of the breed has done much to discourage such abuse.

Following the establishment of the People's Republic of China as a communist nation, the dog population was virtually wiped out. If not for the efforts of Matgo Law of Hong Kong, the Shar-Pei would not be here today. Due to his dedication to the breed, a small number of Shar-Pei were brought to the United States in the 1960s and early 1970s. In 1974, American and Canadian fanciers answered Matgo's appeal for help, and, in 1976, the first Shar-Pei was registered. The foundation stock brought over from Hong Kong were of poorer quality than the Shar-Pei we see today. In August 1991, the Shar-Pei officially completed the requirements for recognition by the American Kennel Club and was placed in the Non-Sporting Group. In 1992, the Canadian Kennel Club also officially recognized and grouped the Shar-Pei in group 6, Non-Sporting events. Since that time, several Shar-Pei are now and are continuing to become CKC and AKC champions.

Over 100,000 Shar Pei exist in the United States and Canada. This unique breed is also recognized by the FCI, HKKC, and the CSPCGB. The CSPCGB operates independently, receiving no input or influence from the UK Kennel Club. The FCI recognizes the HKKC standard, which is based on the traditional type, and not the AKC's Western modified type at this time, as per its general policy of using the standard from the country of the breed's origin.

Description

Appearance

Small, triangular ears, a muzzle shaped like that of a hippopotamus, and a high-set tail also give the Shar Pei a unique look. For show standard, "the tail is thick and round at the base, tapering to a fine point" (AKC standard February 28, 1998).

Colors

Western Shar Pei come in many different colors, such as fawn, red (rose), sand, cream, black, lilac and blue. They resemble the Chow Chow due to having the same blue-black tongue. There are over sixteen recognized colors in AKC. The coat must be solid in color, and any Shar-Pei with a "flowered coat" (spotted) or black and tan in coloration (i.e. German Shepherd) is a disqualification. Colors include black, cream, fawn, red-fawn, red, sable, apricot, chocolate, isabella, and blue. The nose may be black or brick (pink with black), with or without a black mask. A Shar-Pei can also have what is called a "dilute" coloration. Meaning the nose, nails and anus of the dog is the same color as the coat, (i.e. chocolate coat with chocolate nose, nails and anus). All of these color variations are acceptable and beautiful, but the coat color must be solid and well blended throughout the whole body of the dog.

Coat

Western Shar Pei comes in three different coat types: horse, brush and bear coat. The unusual horse coat is rough to the touch, extremely prickly and off-standing and is closer to the original traditional Shar Pei breed in appearance and coat type than the brush or bear coat. This coat is fairly prickly and can be rough or irritating when petting in the opposite direction of the fur. The horse coat is generally thought to be more active and predisposed to dominant behaviour than the brush coat. The brush-coated variety have slightly longer hair and a smoother feel to them. The brush coat is generally considered to be more of a "couch potato" than the horse coat.

Unlike the two coat types above, the bear coat does not meet breed standards and, therefore, cannot be shown. The coat is so much longer than the brush and horse coats that, in most cases, one can not see the famous wrinkles. A bear coat can occur in any litter. Bearcoats are not due to the addition of other breeds, Bearcoats were actually the Elite part of the breed owned mostly by wealthy aristocrats in China prior to Mao's cultural revolution and the first to be exterminated by the regime for being considered bourgeois. "Sand Skin" or Short haired examples of the breed were owned by the peasant class, and were the only survivors of the extermination by the government, but fortunately the Bearcoat gene was present in most horse coats. These short haired versions were used for working dogs and fighting dogs due to their loose skin (although the breed did not have the heart for fighting and was soon replaced by more aggressive breeds). Bearcoats can be seen in Chinese art throughout history, and are considered to be one of the oldest breeds on earth.

This breed has little to no shedding (see Moult).

The Chinese Shar-Pei is a unique and intelligent dog most often recognized for its wrinkles. Initially developed as a Chinese fighting dog, the breed does well today in obedience, agility, herding and tracking, with skills that would have been needed on the farm. Because the name *Shar-Pei* means "sand coat", harshness is a distinctive feature in its two accepted coat types, either horse (short) or brush (up to an inch long). Other unique qualities include black mouth pigment, a slightly "hippo-like" head shape, small ears, deep-set eyes and rising topline.

All Shar-Pei, but especially the horse coat, need early socialization with children, strangers, and other animals. Like other fighting breeds, they can be stubborn, strong-willed and very territorial. Early training can help control these traits before they become problem behaviors. Some people may experience a sensitivity to the harshness of the coat of either length. This is a mild, short-lived rash that can develop on the skin that has been in contact with the coat, most commonly on the forearms.

The brush coat matures early to be a stocky strong dog; therefore, early socialization and training are essential in order to have a dog that is a good family member as well as a welcome member of society. The brush coat is not always as active as the horse coat and are often more content to laze around the house. Like their horse-coat brothers, they are strong-willed, stubborn and territorial, but these are often exhibited to a lesser degree.

Any coat longer than one inch at the withers is called a "bear coat" and is not considered breed standard, as it only occurs when both the male and female carry recessive coat genes. This coat length resembles the coat of the Chow Chow. The personality of the bear coat is very much like that of a brush coat.

Wrinkles

Shar Pei usually come in two varieties. One is covered in large folds of wrinkles, even into adulthood (the Western type and mainly brush coat). The other variation has skin that appears tighter on its body, with wrinkles just on the face and at the withers (the original type and horse coat).

Scientists from the Department of Genome Sciences at the University of Washington, Seattle, announced in January 2010 that they had analysed the genetic code of 10 different pedigree dog breeds. In the Shar-pei they discovered four small differences located in the gene HAS2 which is responsible for making hyaluronic acid synthase 2. That enzyme makes hyaluronic acid, which is one of the key components of the skin. There have been rare cases in which a mutation of the same gene has caused severe wrinkling in humans as well.

Temperament

The Shar Pei is often suspicious of strangers, which pertains to their origin as a guard dog. In general, the breed has proved itself to be a loving, devoted family dog. They are also a very independent and reserved breed. Nevertheless, the Shar Pei is extremely devoted, loyal and affectionate to its family and is amenable to accepting strangers given time and proper introduction at a young age. If poorly socialized or trained, it can become especially territorial and aggressive. Even friendly and well-socialized individuals will retain the breed's watch dog proclivities (such as barking at strangers). It is a largely silent breed, barking only when playing or when worried. The Shar Pei were originally bred as palace guards in China. This breed is also very protective of its home and family, a powerful dog that is willing to guard its family members. The breed is amenable to training but can get bored from repetition. Overall, the Shar Pei is a dog that is loyal and loving to its family while being very protective and independent.

Health

Because of its fame after being introduced to North America in the 1970s, the breed suffered much inexperienced or rushed breeding. This resulted not only in a dramatically different look for the Shar-Pei (as its most distinctive features, including its wrinkles and rounded snout, were greatly exaggerated), but also in a large number of health problems that are still slowly being worked out of the breed today.

Allergy-induced skin infections can be a problem in this breed, caused by poorly selected breeding stock. This has become rarer over the years with responsible breeders and lines.

Familial Shar Pei fever (FSF) is a serious congenital disease that causes short fevers lasting up to 24 hours, usually accompanied by accumulation of fluid around the ankles (called Swollen Hock Syndrome). These fevers may or may not recur at more frequent intervals and become more intense. Amyloidosis, a long-term condition, is most likely related to FSF, caused by unprocessed amyloid proteins depositing in the organs, most often in the kidneys or liver, leading eventually to renal failure. There is no early test for FSF, but as it is congenital, the dog is either born with it or without it, and if one attack occurs (usually brought on by excessive emotional or physical stress), the dog will always be susceptible to another. With proper care, a Shar-Pei with FSF can live a completely normal and long life.

A common problem is a painful eye condition, entropion, in which the eyelashes curl inward, irritating the eye. Untreated, it can cause blindness. This condition can be fixed by surgery ("tacking" the eyelids up so they will not roll onto the eyeball for puppies or surgically removing extra skin in adolescent and older Shar Pei).

Chinese Shar Pei can be notoriously allergic to food products that contain soy, corn, wheat, gluten or sugars (or can develop these allergies without proper care early on). It is recommended in the breed now to use a completely grain-free food to offset and try to prevent these allergies. Often, the consumption of these types of poor-quality foods result in allergic skin reactions. Shar Pei whose food intake is restricted to better-quality foods free of corn, soy, wheat, and gluten will enjoy much healthier lives with little or no skin irritation, itching, or sores.

Responsible breeders work with great success to reduce the frequency of these genetic problems, and so finding an experienced, well-established Shar-Pei breeder is important. Some problems (i.e., the need for eye tacking) can be virtually eliminated from experienced breeders' litters. The breeder will also give the best and most detailed diet information specific to their Shar-Pei.

History

The Shar Pei breed comes from the Guangdong province of China. The original Shar-Pei from China looked very different from the breed now popular in the West. People in southern China, Hong Kong, and Macau differentiate the Western type and the original type by calling them respectively "meat-mouth" and "bone-mouth" Shar-Pei.

The ancestry of the Shar-Pei is uncertain. It may be a descendant of the Chow Chow; however, the only clear link between these is the blue-black tongue. However, pictures on pottery suggest the breed was present even in the Han Dynasty (206 BC). For many years, the Shar-Pei was kept as a general-purpose farm dog in the Chinese countryside, used for hunting, protecting and herding stock and guarding the home and family. During that time, the Shar-Pei was bred for intelligence, strength and scowling face.

Later, it was used for dog fighting. The loose skin and extremely prickly coat were developed originally to help the Shar Pei fend off wild boar, as they were used to hunt. Dog fighters used these enhanced traits to make the Shar-Pei difficult for its opponent to grab and hold on to, and so that if it did manage to hold on, the Shar-Pei would still have room to maneuver and bite back. The Shar-Pei's most intriguing feature, in this respect, is that if one grabs them by any loose wrinkle, they can actually twist in their skin and face in one's direction. This trait was used in fighting as a means for them to fight back; they would be bitten and twist in their skin to bite back at the offender. During the Communist Revolution, when the Shar Pei population dwindled dramatically, dogs were rescued by a Hong Kong businessman named Matgo Law, who appealed to Americans in 1973 through a dog magazine to save the breed. Around 200 Shar-Peis were smuggled into America. The current American Shar Pei population stems mainly from these original 200.

DNA analysis has concluded that the Shar Pei is one of the most ancient dog breeds.

Famous Shar-Pei

- Lao-Tzu, Martin Prince's dog in *The Simpsons*, appeared in two episodes: "Bart's Dog Gets an F" and "Two Dozen and One Greyhounds".
- Fu Dog from the Disney cartoon *American Dragon: Jake Long* is a Shar Pei.
- Satchel, from the syndicated comic strip *Get Fuzzy*, is half yellow lab and half Shar Pei.
- Malcolm and Derek, from the TV version of *Creature Comforts*.
- A Shar Pei appears in the television show *Lost* as character Sun Kwon's pet, Bpo Bpo.
- In a British television advert for a Garnier anti-wrinkle cream, a Shar Pei puppy is featured.
- New Kids on the Block member Jonathan Knight had a Shar Pei named Nikko that went on tour with him and appeared in many magazine articles and pictures focused on the group.
- In Australia and New Zealand, a Shar Pei puppy named Roly has been used for many years in television commercials for Purex toilet paper.
- Popeye, a Shar Pei dog that appeared in Hong Kong TVB comedy shows.
- Zac Lichman from *Big Brother* had a Shar Pei named Molly, who undertook a task on Day 55 and was also reunited.
- Alfie, a Shar Pei from Essex owned by the Seaton-Collins family, best known for winning the Crufts 2006 gold show dog award.
- G-Dragon from the popular Korean hip-hop group Big Bang has a Shar Pei puppy named Gaho. Gaho is featured several times in a documentary, *GDTV*, from Mnet.
- On 30 March 2010, ex-soccer player and now manager Diego Maradona suffered a bite to his lip from a Shar Pei dog owned by his family.

See also

- List of dog fighting breeds
- Foo Dog, dog breeds originating in China that resemble Chinese guardian lions and hence are also called Foo or Fu Dogs or Lion Dogs

External links

- Shar Pei breed overview by Complete Dogs Guide [1]
- More on the traditional Bone-mouth Shar-pei [2]
- Information on the Shar-pei, its ancestry, care and training [3]

Chow Chow

Chow chow, or **chow**, is a breed of dog that was first developed in Mongolia about 4,000 years ago and was later introduced into China, where it is referred to as *Songshi Quan* (Pinyin: sōngshī quǎn 鬆獅犬), which literally means "puffy-lion dog".

Appearance

The chow is a sturdily built dog that is square in profile with broad skull and small, triangular, erect ears that are rounded at the tip. The breed has a very dense double coat that is either smooth or rough. The fur is particularly thick around the neck, giving the distinctive ruff or mane appearance. The coat may be one of five colors including red, black, blue, cinnamon/fawn, and cream. Their eyes should be deep set and almond in shape. Chows are distinguished by their unusual blue-black/purple tongue and very straight hind legs, resulting in a rather stilted gait. The bluish color extends to the chow's lips, which is the only dog breed with this distinctive bluish appearance in its lips and oral cavity (other dogs have black or a piebald pattern skin in their mouths). One other distinctive feature is their curly tail. It has thick hair and lies curled on its back. Their nose should be black (except the blue which can have a solid blue or slate colored nose). Any other tone is disqualification for showing in the United States under AKC breed standard. However, FCI countries do allow for a self-colored nose in the cream.

The blue-black/purple tongue gene appears to be dominant, as almost all mixed breed dogs that come from a chow retain the tongue color. This is not to say, however, that every mixed breed dog with spots of purple on the tongue is descended from chows as purple spots on the tongue can be found on a multitude of pure breed dogs.

Temperament

Today the chow chow is most commonly kept as a pet. Its keen sense of proprietorship over its home, paired with a sometimes disconcertingly serious approach to strangers, can be off-putting to those unfamiliar with the breed. However, displays of timidity and aggression are uncharacteristic of well-bred and well-socialized specimens. The chow is extremely loyal to its own family and will bond tightly to its master. The chow typically shows affection only with those it has bonds to, so new visitors to the home should not press their physical attention upon the resident chow as it will not immediately accept strangers in the same manner as it does members of its own pack. Inexperienced dog owners should beware of how chow chows encounter those it perceives as strangers; their notoriety is so established that many homeowner's insurance companies will not cover dogs from this breed. Males and females typically co-habitate with less tension than those of the same gender, but it is not unheard of for multiple chows of both genders to live together peacefully in a home setting.

Chows are not a particularly active breed. Apartment life can suit them, if they are given enough opportunity for regularly-scheduled physical activity each day. The chow chow may appear to be independent and aloof for much of the day, keeping a comfortable distance from others while staying within earshot, or preferring to watch for strangers alone by the entrance. Owners still need to be prepared to take a chow chow for a brisk daily walk, even if they have a fenced yard, in order to meet the dog's needs for mental and physical stimulation. While the chow exhibits low energy for most of the day, it will crave routine time to explore and play to maintain a happy and content disposition. They rank 77th in Stanley Coren's The Intelligence of Dogs, being of the lowest degree of working/obedience intelligence. However, most chow owners believe this is because the chow has a different type of intelligence than that found in most dogs. Many chows excel with positive reinforcement methods of training, particularly "Clicker Training", as the chow is a natural problem solver and gets bored with endless, repetitive tasks. Unless the chow is kept engaged, boredom sets in and the chow will simply walk away or refuse to engage.

Health

The chow chow is the dog breed most affected by elbow dysplasia. It is also prone to hip dysplasia, patellar luxation (slipping knee caps), thyroid disease, pemphigus foliaceus and ocular disorders such as entropion and ectropion. The risk of such disorders increases exponentially when a chow is purchased from backyard breeders, pet stores and unscrupulous kennels that do not test their breeding stock for such genetic disorders. Thus, a potential chow buyer should ask to see all health clearances for the parents of a litter up front. In the United States, these would be clearances from the Canine Eye Registration Foundation and Orthopedic Foundation for Animals; other countries will have other health testing schemes, and contacting the national canine registry association will provide that information. Reputable kennels should provide the new owner with a written and signed health warranty as well. Although there is no way to accurately predict the lifespan of an animal, one should expect the healthy chow to live between 10 to 15 years.

History

Recent DNA analysis confirms that the chow chow is one of the oldest breeds of dog. Research indicates it is one of the first primitive breeds to evolve from the wolf, and is thought to have originated in the arid steppes of northern China/Mongolia. A Chinese bas-relief from 150 BC shows a hunting dog and a dog very friendly toward children similar in appearance to the chow. Later, chow chows were bred as general-purpose working dogs for hunting, herding, pulling and protection of the home. The black tongued chow was also bred for human consumption. Some scholars claim the chow was the original ancestor of the samoyed, norwegian elkhound, pomeranian and keeshond .

In the United States, the chow chow was a highly popular pet among the rich and famous during the Roaring Twenties. President Calvin Coolidge and his wife owned a black chow named Timmy. Chow chows were also popular in the 1930s and 1980s.

Etymology of Chow Name

In the early 1800s, clipper ships sailed from China to England, bringing back a various assortment of cargo, referred to as chow chow. These miscellaneous objects were stored in the ship's hold called the chow chow hold, chow chow meaning bits and pieces of this and that. The first chow chow dog appeared in England in the 1830s, and was known as the chow chow dog because he had been housed in the chow chow hold during the long voyage.

See also

- Foo Dog

External links

- The Chow Chow Club, Inc. [1]
- The Netherlands Chow Chow Club [2]
- The Royal Belgian Chow Chow Club [3]
- Quality Dogs - Chow Chow Information [4]

Dalmatian (dog)

The **Dalmatian** () is a breed of dog whose roots are traced to Dalmatia, a region of Croatia. It is noted for its white coat with either black or liver spots.

Appearance

Body

This popular breed of dog is a well-muscled, mid-sized, elegant dog with excellent endurance and stamina. The Dalmatian is slightly longer than tall according to the European (FCI) standard. The American Kennel Club standard states that the dog should be more square, as long from forechest to buttocks as it is tall at the withers. Shoulder should be well laid back and rear angulation should match the front with the stifle well-bent indicating good angulation in the rear. The feet are round and compact with well-arched toes. The nails are white and/or the same color as the spots. The ears are thin, tapering toward the tip, set fairly high and carried close to the head.

Size

The breed standard for Dalmatians varies slightly from country to country, with the FCI allowing a larger dog than does the AKC. In general, the height for the Dalmatian is between 19 and 24 inches (48.5 and 61.5 cm) at the withers and the weight is from 35 to 70 lb (16 to 32 kg) fully grown. Males are usually larger than females.

Coat

The Dalmatian coat is short, fine, and dense. Dalmatians shed considerably, and shed year-round. The short, stiff hairs shed by Dalmatians will weave their way into clothing, upholstery and nearly any other kind of fabric. While consistent grooming with a hound mitt or curry can lessen the amount of hair that Dalmatians shed, nothing can completely prevent the shedding.

Occasionally, smooth-coated Dalmatians will produce long-coated offspring who shed less often. These dogs are still purebred Dalmatians but cannot be shown.

Colouring

Dalmatian puppies are born white, and their spots come in gradually over the period of a couple of weeks.

The most common colours for Dalmatians are black or liver spotted on a white background. Other spotting colors, although rare and not permitted for showing, include blue (a blue-grayish color), orange or lemon (dark to pale yellow), brindle, mosaic, and tri-colored (with tan spotting on the eyebrows, cheeks, legs, and chest).

Patches often occur in the breed and are a disqualification in the show ring. Patches are present at birth, and consist of a solid color. Patches can appear anywhere on the body, but are most common on the head and ears. Patches are not to be confused with heavily spotted areas on a dog, however. Spots should be in size of a quarter to half-dollar.

Eye colour in Dalmatians is brown, amber, or blue. Dalmatians may have one blue eye and one brown eye. While blue eyes are accepted by the AKC, blue eyes are regarded as a fault in many kennel clubs. The CKC faults any eye color other than black, brown or amber, and the Kennel Club (UK) allows only dark eyes in black-spotted dogs, and amber eyes in liver-spotted dogs.

Temperament

The Dalmatian is incredibly loyal and active. Usually good with other pets, notably horses, dalmatians make an excellent addition to a family that already has animals of any kind.They usually aren't the best with children under ten, but regular training may help. Dalmatians are a rather active breed, and strongly dislike lazing around with nothing to do, however they will be thrilled to go for walks, or runs, and play with an active owner. Dalmatians are known for their loyal nature and thrive on human companionship. Dalmatians are occasionally known to have a stubborn streak, but are revered for their excellent memories. Dalmatians need to be handled and socialized from a young age to prevent timidity, which if not addressed properly may result in aggression out of fear. Though this is rare, it is universal that dalmatians need love and companionship from a young age. If given exercise, love, training, and socialization a dalmatian will be tirelessly loyal and affectionate.

Uses

The dalmatian is very powerful, but high-strung and potentially difficult to train. Its boundless energy makes it great for a rescue dog, or an athletic partner, or active family member.

History

The FCI recognized as its country of origin the region of Dalmatia in the Republic of Croatia, citing Bewick's 1792 work.

The Republic of Croatia was recognized by the F.C.I. as the country of origin of the Dalmatian; the breed had been developed and cultivated chiefly in England. When the dog with the distinctive markings was first shown in England in 1862 it was said to have been used by the frontier guards of Dalmatia as a guard dog. But nothing is definitely known about its origin. The breed has become widely distributed over the continent of Europe since 1920. Its unusual markings were often mentioned by the old writers on cynology.

The duties of this ancient breed are as varied as their reputed ancestors. They were used as dogs of war, guarding the borders of Dalmatia. To this day, the breed retains a high guarding instinct; although friendly and loyal to those the dog knows and trusts, it is often aloof with strangers and unknown dogs. Dalmatians have a strong hunting instinct and are an excellent exterminator of rats and vermin. In sporting, they have been used as bird dogs, trail hounds, retrievers, or in packs for boar or stag hunting. Their dramatic markings and intelligence have made them successful circus dogs throughout the years. Dalmatians are perhaps best known for their role as a fire-apparatus follower and as a firehouse mascot.

However, the Dalmatian's most important task has been his role as a coach or carriage dog, so called because they were formerly used to run in attendance of a coach. To this day, Dalmatians retain a strong affinity for horses, often naturally falling in behind a horse and cart in perfect position. The strong-bodied, clean-cut and athletic build of the Dalmatians reflects their years as a coach dog, although they are rarely used in this capacity today. Their physical make-up is still ideally suited to road work. Like its ancestors, the modern Dalmatian is an energetic dog, with unlimited energy and stamina.

Association with firefighters

Particularly in the United States, the use of Dalmatians as carriage dogs was transferred to horse-drawn fire engines, although it is unclear why this link was not made in other countries. Today the Dalmatian serves as a firehouse mascot but, back in the days of horse-drawn fire carts, they provided a valuable service. Dalmatians and horses are very compatible, so the dogs were easily trained to run in front of the carriages to help clear a path and quickly guide the horses and firefighters to the fires. Dalmatians are often considered to make good watchdogs and it is believed that Dalmatians may have been useful to fire brigades as guard dogs to protect a firehouse and its equipment. Fire engines used to be drawn by fast and powerful horses, a tempting target for thieves, so Dalmatians were kept in the firehouse as deterrence to theft. The horses have long since gone, but the Dalmatians, by tradition, have stayed. As a result, in the United States, Dalmatians are commonly known as firehouse dogs. Dalmatians are still chosen by many firefighters as pets, in honor of their heroism in the past.

The Dalmatian is also associated, particularly in the United States, with Budweiser beer and the Busch Gardens theme parks, since the Anheuser-Busch company's iconic beer wagon, drawn by a team of Clydesdale horses, is always accompanied by a Dalmatian carriage dog. The company maintains several teams at various locations, which tour extensively. According to Anheuser-Busch's website,

Dalmatians were historically used by brewers to guard the wagon while the driver was making deliveries.

Health

Like other breeds, Dalmatians display a propensity towards certain health problems. Hip dysplasia (which affects only 4.6% of purebred Dalmatians) is not a major issue in this breed. Most of their health problems result from the onset of old age; the average Dalmatian lives between 12 and 14 years, although some can live as long as 17 to 18 years. In their late teens, both males and females may suffer bone spurs and arthritic conditions. Autoimmune thyroiditis is a relatively common condition for the breed affecting 10.4% of dogs.

Deafness

A genetic predisposition for deafness is a serious health problem for Dalmatians, only approximately 70% of Dalmatians having normal hearing. Deafness was not recognized by early breeders, so the breed was thought to be unintelligent. Even after recognizing the problem as a genetic fault, breeders did not understand the dog's nature, and deafness in Dalmatians continues to be a frequent problem.

Researchers now know that deafness in albino and piebald animals is caused by the absence of mature melanocytes in the inner ear. This may affect one or both ears. The condition is also common in other canine breeds that share a genetic propensity for light pigmentation. This includes, but is not limited to bull terriers, Poodles, boxers, border collies and Great Danes.

Similarly, Charles Darwin commented on the tendency of white, blue-eyed cats to be deaf, while Waardenburg syndrome is the human analog. There is an accurate test called the BAER test, which can determine if the defect is present. Puppies can be tested beginning at five weeks of age. BAER testing is the only way of detecting unilateral deafness, and reputable breeders test their dogs prior to breeding.

Only dogs with bilateral hearing should be allowed to breed, although those with unilateral hearing, and even dogs with bilateral deafness, make fine pets with appropriate training. Research shows that Dalmatians with large patches of color present at birth have a lower rate of deafness, and breeding for this trait, which is currently prohibited in the breed standard, might reduce the frequency of deafness in the breed. One of the leading reasons patches are a disqualifying factor in Dalmatians is to preserve the much prized spotted coat—the continual breeding of patched dogs would result in heavily patched Dalmatians with few spots.

Research concludes that blue-eyed Dalmatians have a greater incidence of deafness than brown-eyed Dalmatians, although an absolute link between the two characteristics has yet to be conclusively proven. Though blue-eyed Dalmatians are not necessarily deaf, many kennel clubs consider blue eyes to be a fault or even a disqualification, and some discourage the use of blue-eyed Dalmatians in breeding programs.

Bladder stones

Dalmatians, like humans, the great apes, some New World monkeys, and guinea pigs, can suffer from hyperuricemia. The latter lack an enzyme called uricase, which breaks down uric acid. However, in Dalmatians, the deficit seems to be in liver transport. Uric acid can build up in the blood serum (hyperuricemia), causing gout; and can be excreted in high concentration into the urine, causing kidney stones and bladder stones. These conditions are most likely to occur in middle-aged males. Males over 10 are prone to kidney stones and should have calcium intake reduced or take preventive medication.

To reduce the risk of gout and stones, owners should be careful to limit the intake of purine by not feeding these dogs organ meats, animal by-products, or other high-purine ingredients. Hyperuricemic syndrome in Dalmatians responds to treatment with Orgotein, the veterinary formulation of the antioxidant enzyme superoxide dismutase.

In one family of these dogs, a genetic mutation has been reported that contributes to hypouricemia (although hyeruricosuria remains).

Crosses to English Pointers

Hyperuricemia in Dalmatians (as in all breeds) is inherited. However, unlike other breeds of dog the "normal" gene for uricase is not present in the breed's gene pool at all. Therefore, there is no possibility of eliminating hyperuricemia among pure-bred Dalmatians. The only possible solution to this problem must then be crossing Dalmatians with other breeds in order to reintroduce the "normal" uricase gene.

This has led to the foundation of the "Dalmatian-Pointer Backcross Project", which aims to reintroduce the normal uricase gene into the Dalmatian breed. The backcross that was done was to a single English pointer; subsequent breedings have all been to purebred Dalmatians. This project was started in 1973 by Dr. Robert Schaible. The f1 hybrids did not resemble Dalmatians very closely. The f1s were then crossed back to pure-bred Dals. This breeding produced puppies of closer resemblance to the pure Dal. By the fifth generation in 1981 they resembled pure Dals so much that Dr. Schaible convinced the AKC to allow two of the hybrids to be registered along with pure-bred Dals. Then AKC President William F. Stifel stated that "If there is a logical, scientific way to correct genetic health problems associated with certain breed traits and still preserve the integrity of the breed standard, it is incumbent upon the American Kennel Club to lead the way." The Dalmatian Club of America's (DCA) board of directors supported this decision, however it quickly became highly controversial among the club members. A vote by DCA members opposed the registration of the hybrids, causing the AKC to ban registration to any of the dog's offspring.

At the annual general meeting of the DCA in May 2006 the backcross issue was discussed again by club members. In June of the same year DCA members were presented with an opportunity to vote on whether to reopen discussion of the Dalmatian Backcross Project. The results of this ballot were nearly 2:1 in favor of re-examining support of the Dalmatian Backcross Project by the Dalmatian Club of America. This has begun with publication of articles presenting more information both in support of and questioning the need for this Project. As of May 2007, discussion is on-going.

In January 2010, the UK Kennel Club announced its decision to register a backcrossed Dalmatian, pending confirmation of the dog's appearance and characteristics by two Championship Show judges. The decision was made due to the club's "commitment to consider applications to register dogs from out-crossings and inter-variety matings if it is felt that to do so may present potential health and welfare benefits." Several restrictions were imposed on the dog. Although the dog is at least 13 generations removed from the original Pointer cross, its F1 to F3 progeny will be marked on registration certificates with asterisks (which "indicate impure or unverified breeding"), no progeny will be eligible to be exported as pedigrees for the next five years, and all have to be health tested.

Popularity

The Dalmatian breed experienced a massive surge in popularity as a result of the 1956 novel *The Hundred and One Dalmatians* written by British author Dodie Smith, and later due to the two Walt Disney films based on the book. The Disney animated classic released in 1961, later spawned a 1996 live-action remake, *101 Dalmatians*. In the years following the release of the second movie, the Dalmatian breed suffered greatly at the hands of irresponsible breeders and inexperienced owners.

Many well-meaning enthusiasts purchased Dalmatians—often for their children—without educating themselves on the breed and the responsibilities that come with owning such a high-energy dog breed. Since Dalmatians were originally bred to run with horses, they require frequent exercise to keep them out of mischief. Many owners find themselves unable to cope with the breed's or the specimen's characteristics and cannot provide their dogs with adequate care. Dalmatians were abandoned in large numbers by their original owners and left with animal shelters. As a result, Dalmatian rescue organizations sprung up to care for the unwanted dogs and find them new homes. There was a 90% decrease in AKC registrations of dalmatians during the 2000-2010 period.

Famous Dalmatians

- **Pongo, Mrs. Pongo/Missus, Perdita, Prince (Perdita's Mate)**, and their puppies in *The Hundred and One Dalmatians* and its derivative works (The Starlight Barking, etc.).
- Sparky the Fire Dog Mascot of the American National Fire Protection Association.
- Louie (Lou Dog), the mascot of the band Sublime, owned by singer Bradley Nowell.
- Budweiser Dalmatian, the mascot along with BUD (the horse) for Anheuser Busch Budweiser Brewery
- Spottie Dottie
- Friar Boy, a series of dalmatian mascots for the Providence College Friars (the Dalmatian is also the mascot of the Dominican Order)

See also

- Companion dog
- Companion Dog Group
- Utility Group
- Non-Sporting Group
- Rajapalayam (dog)

External links

- Dalmatian-Pointer Backcross Project [1]
- British Carriage Dog Society [2]
- Dalmatian Club of America [3]
- Dalmatian Color Variations [4]
- All About Dalmatians [5] (Trivia)
- Deafness in Dogs: LSU & Dr. Strain [6]
- http://www.aboutdalmatians.com

Finnish Spitz

A **Finnish Spitz** (Finnish language: *Suomenpystykorva*) is a breed of dog originating in Finland. The breed is thought to be an old one, bred as a hunting dog. It is a "bark pointer", indicating the position of game by barking to attract the hunter's attention. It has been used mostly to bark at game that flees into trees, such as squirrels, grouses, and capercaillies, but it serves well also to hunt moose and elk. Some individuals have been known to go after even a bear, despite the dog's small size. In its native country, the breed is still mostly used as a hunting dog, but as it is very friendly and loves children, in other countries it serves mainly as a house pet. The Finnish Spitz has been the national dog of Finland since 1979.

Descriptions

Appearance

The Finnish Spitz has a square build, meaning that the length of the body is the same, or slightly shorter than the height of the withers to the ground. It should look like a fox with a fluffier coat. The length of the body is measured from the point of the shoulder or forechest in front of the withers to the rump, giving a truly square dogs a short back. Females are usually a little longer in the back. Both dogs and females should appear slightly longer in the leg. The Finnish Spitz is a double coated breed but the outer coat should not exceed 2½ inches at the ruff. The undercoat is soft and lighter in color than the red/gold outer coat. The undercoat will shed twice a year, and if a Finnish Spitz is to be kept healthy, a good shedding of the undercoat when the dog is ready to "blow coat" is needed. Some exhibitors show dogs with undercoat that should be removed but that is the breeder, owner or handler's choice. Omission to shed undercoat is considered neglect by some judges who prefer a clean and combed coat. Dew claws can appear on front and/or back feet. If back claws appear, they should be removed by the breeder. The front dewclaws can be removed but since they are usually small, they generally are not removed. If the back dew claws are present, they look like toes. The front dew claws appear to have no purpose.

Coat

The Finnish Spitz has a typical double coat, which consists of a soft, dense undercoat and long, harsh guard hairs that can measure one to two inches long. The coat should be stiffer, denser, and longer on the neck, back, back of thighs, and plume of the tail, whilst shorter on the head and legs. Dogs should sport a slightly longer and coarser coat than the bitches, who are slightly more refined. However the plume of the tail is important to the overall look of the dog but should not be too long. Feathered long tail hairs without sustenance can give the dog an unkempt look. Additionally the tailset is important and the Finnish Spitz should be able to move its tail from one side to the other. Most Finnish Spitz have a preferred side and this is not incorrect.

Proper care of the coat is most important. The Finnish Spitz blows coat or loses its undercoat twice a year. It is imperative that owners brush out the old undercoat so the new coat can grow properly. Excessive undercoat can cause skin problems and although a dog may look fluffy and full, the undercoat may be causing serious skin problems.

In the show ring, the coat should be shown as completely natural; a brush through the coat is acceptable but no trimming is allowed, not even of whiskers. However, any excessive undercoat should be removed. Some exhibitors leave in the undercoat to make the dog's coat look bigger. However, most well trained judges see this problem. Another exception is the hair under the bottom of the feet. The hair under the feet as well as the toe nails should be nicely trimmed for show.

Color

Puppies are often described as looking similar to a red fox cub. They are born dark grey/black/brown or fawn with a vast amount of black. A fawn puppy or one with a large amount of white of the chest is not preferable. The color of the adult dog can be assessed by an experienced breeder at birth or cannot really be assessed by a novice until about four to six months, but even then the color may change. The adult color should be golden red. It can be of almost any shade, varying from pale honey to dark chestnut. There are no preferences over shades as long as the color is bright and clear with no hints of dullness, which is of most importance. The coat should never be of a solid color. It should be shaded and without any defined color changes. The coat is usually at its darkest shade on the back of the dog, gradually getting lighter around the chest and belly. The undercoat must always be lighter in color than the topcoat, but is never allowed to be white. A small patch of white, no more than 1.5 centimeters wide, is allowable on the chest, and white tips on the feet are acceptable, but not desired.

Pigmentation

The nose, lips, and rims of eyes should always be black.

Height and weight

- Height at withers

    Males, 16 to 19 inches (44–50 cm)

    Females, 14½ to 17 inches (39–45 cm)

- Weight

    Males, 47-53 lb (11–13 kg)

    Females, 40-47 lb (8–9 kg)

Temperament

Finnish Spitz are considered to interact well with people, including children. In the home, the Finnish Spitz is a happy member, playing gently with children, but may be rougher with other dogs. Some Finnish Spitz love other dogs while others are shy, passive, or aggressive around them. Left alone the Finnish Spitz will figure out if another canine is acceptable.

The breed is prone to barking at anything they perceive as being out of the ordinary. They can be trained to reduce the amount of barking, although the barking does make them good watchdogs.

Training

Because of their intelligence, Finnish Spitz are independent and strong-willed dogs and are best trained with a soft voice and touch. They will easily become bored with repetitive training. Finnish Spitz can be trained to be very obedient with a light touch and lots of positive reinforcement.

Finnish Spitz can excel in obedience, agility and rally as a companion dog.

Health

The Finnish Spitz is typically a very healthy breed, and health concerns are rare. Here is a short list of what is known to occur. However, you should consult your breeder and others who breed Finnish Spitz to understand the prevalence to this breed.

- Hip dysplasia
- Patellar luxation
- Elbow dysplasia
- Epilepsy

References

- The American Kennel Club official site [1]
- The Finnish Spitz club of America [2]
- The Finnish Spitz Directory [3]
- History, Breed information [4]
- FinnishSpitzOnline.com
  - Brief breed history [5]
  - Breed information [6]

French Bulldog

The **French Bulldog** is a small companion breed of dog. The name suggests that France is the country of origin, but, in fact, the Americans and British may have played a larger role in the breed's development. The dogs are commonly called the **Frenchie** and are nicknamed "clowns" and "frog dogs".

Physical description

French bulldogs are a compact companion dog, active but not sporty. They are muscular dogs with a smooth coat, snub nose and solid bone structure. Their physical appearance is characterized by naturally occurring "bat ears" that are wide at the base and rounded at the top. Their tails are naturally short, not cropped, and can be straight or screwed, but not curly.

Under the American Kennel Club and Canadian Kennel Club standards, weight is not to exceed 28 pounds (13 kg). In general, French bulldogs range in weight from 22 to 30 pounds. The Fédération Cynologique Internationale (FCI) does not set a strict weight limit, simply stating "The weight must not be below 8 kg nor over 14 kg for a bulldog in good condition, size being in proportion with the weight".

Coat and colors in French bulldogs

French bulldogs come in a variety of colors and coat patterns. Including cream, brindle, black, white, red, fawn, blue and chocolate brown. The dog may also have any of those colous when it is pied.

The FCI standard for French Bulldogs is shown at [www.fci.be/nomenclature.aspx], and disqualifies brown, black and tan, and mouse grey colorings.

Temperament

The French Bulldog is a gentle breed that typically has a happy-go-lucky attitude. Like many other companion dog breeds they require close contact with humans. They have fairly minimal exercise needs, but do require at least daily walks. Their calm nature makes them excellent choices for apartment dwellers, as does their usually sensible attitude towards barking. As a flat faced breed, it is essential that owners understand that French Bulldogs cannot live outdoors. Their bulk and their compromised breathing system makes it impossible for them to regulate their temperature efficiently. In addition, Frenchies are top heavy and therefore have a difficult time swimming. Precautions must be taken when exercising a Frenchie during hot or humid weather, as well.

French Bulldogs can play too roughly for some smaller children, and should be monitored at all times during play. As well, children should be cautioned not to pick French Bulldogs up, as the dogs' small size can mask how heavy they are. They can look unmuscular but in reality they are very strong.

French Bulldogs are essentially a bull and terrier breed, and as such, it is not surprising to learn that canine aggression can sometimes occur. Generally, this takes the form of same sex aggression. Owners considering adding a second dog to their household are usually cautioned to choose one of the opposite sex. Spaying or neutering can do much to curb aggressive tendencies before they begin. The French Bulldog energy level can range from hyperactive and energetic to relaxed and laid back.

Health

There are several congenital diseases and conditions to which French bulldogs are susceptible, although they are still considered among the healthiest of the bull breeds. Frenchies can suffer from Von Willebrand's disease (VWD), a bleeding disorder that is also found in humans and is similar to hemophilia, which can impede their clotting. In conjunction to this, French bulldogs may also suffer from thyroid condition. Many breeders follow a program of testing younger dogs for VWD, and only testing for thyroid at that time if the VWD factor is low. In this program, the breeder tests thyroid again just prior to using the dog for breeding. Other breeders test both VWD and thyroid at the same time.

French bulldogs suffer from brachycephalic syndrome, which is what creates the flat faced appearance of the Frenchie. As a result, one of the most common defects in French bulldogs is elongated soft palate or cleft palate. Puppies affected with Cleft palate are generally put down at birth, as it is generally considered to be an almost impossible condition to correct. Elongated soft palate can manifest as anything from a mild condition causing labored breathing to severe condition that can cause the affected dog to pass out from moderate exercise.

Frenchies may also have a tendency towards eye issues. Cherry eye, or everted third eyelid, has been known to occur, although it is more common in (English) bulldogs and pug dogs. Glaucoma, retinal fold dysplasia, corneal ulcers and juvenile cataracts are also conditions which have been known to afflict French bulldogs. Screening of prospective breeding candidates through CERF - the Canine Eye

Registration Foundation — can help to eliminate instances of these diseases in offpsring. The skin folds under the eyes of the French bulldog must be cleaned regularly and kept dry in order to avoid fold infections. In extremely severe cases of persistent fold infections, some veterinarians have performed fold removal surgeries.

French bulldogs can also suffer from a condition called megaesophagus, a term which collectively describes several esophageal disorders and malformations in any combination from single-to-double or multiple. One of the more serious complications in a dog affected with megaesophagus is passive regurgitation, in which the affected dog vomits up food or phlegm after eating or exercise. Passive regurgitation can frequently result in aspiration pneumonia.

Another result of the compacted airway of the French bulldog is their inability to effectively regulate temperature. While a regular canine may suffer to some degree from the heat, to a Frenchie it may be lethal. It is imperative that they be protected from temperature extremes at all times, and that they always have access to fresh water and shade.

French bulldogs can also suffer from an assortment of back and spinal diseases, most of which are probably related to the fact that they were selectively chosen from the dwarf examples of the bulldog breed. This condition is also referred to as chondrodysplasia. Some breeders feel that only dogs that have been x-rayed and checked for spinal anomalies should be bred from, but this is a difficult position to take sides on. While it is true that no dog affected with a spinal disease should be bred from , there is a great deal of variance in the appearance of a French Bulldog's spine as compared to, for example, a Labrador retriever. If possible, such decisions should be left to either a veterinarian or breeder who has seen quite a few bulldog breed spinal x-rays, to avoid eliminating dogs unnecessarily.

French bulldogs frequently require caesarean section to give birth, with over 80% of litters delivered this way.As well, many French bulldog stud dogs are incapable of naturally breeding, requiring breeders to undertake artificial insemination of bitches (female dogs). French bitches can also suffer from erratic or 'silent' heats, which may be a side effect of thyroid disease or impaired thyroid function.

Thyroid disease may also be responsible for some of the skin conditions which afflict some Frenchies. Skin allergies, obsessive foot licking, and interdigital cysts have been known to affect some French Bulldogs.

Famous French Bulldog

- Alex/Freddy in Fortune Dogs

See also

- Bulldog
- Companion dog
- Companion Dog Group
- Non-Sporting Group
- Utility Group
- Bull and terrier

References

Books:

- Muriel Lee. *The French Bulldog, Kennel Club Classics*, Kennel Club Books, ISBN 1-59378-680-8
- Michael Rosser, A. Winsor D.V.M, A Alford, Jane Flowers. *Celebrating Frenchies*, ARDesign Inc., ISBN 0-9660133-5-2
- Durr-Grebe, Janice. *Flat Face Encyclopedia: Bulldogs and French bulldogs, A to Z*, ARDesign Inc., ISBN 0-9660133-0-1
- Dannel, Kathy. *The French Bulldog: An Owner's Guide to a Happy Healthy Pet*, Barron's Educational Series, ISBN 0-7641-3031-5
- Coile, Dr. Caroline. *French Bulldogs (Complete Pet Owner's Manual)*, Howell Book House, ISBN 1-58245-163-X
- McDonald,Joan. *The Book of the Bulldog*, Neptune, NJ:TFH Publications, ISBN 0-86622-027-5
- Jenkins, Robert. *The Story of the Real Bulldog* Neptune, NJ: TFH Publications, ISBN 0-7938-0491-4

Magazines and manuals:

- French Bulldog Magazine [1], 24+ years in print. The premier magazine for French Bulldog lovers worldwide.
- JustFrenchies Magazine [2], Quarterly breed magazine for French Bulldog fanciers
- Viva Les Frenchies [3], the magazine for every French Bulldog Lover!

Rescue Organizations:

- Bulldog Haven NW [4], Rescue organization for Bulldogs, including Frechies and Frenchie Mixes. Based in WA

Keeshond

The **Keeshond** (, ; plural: **Keeshonden**) is a medium-sized dog with a plush two-layer coat of silver and black fur with a 'ruff' and a curled tail, originating in Germany. Its closest relatives are the other German spitzes such as the Pomeranian. Originally called the **German Spitz**, more specifically the **Wolfsspitz**, the name was officially changed to Keeshond in England, where it had been known as the Dutch Barge Dog, in 1926.

Description

Appearance

A member of the spitz group of dogs, the Keeshond in AKC standard is to tall and ± in the FCI standard and weighs to . Sturdily built, they have a typical spitz appearance, neither coarse nor refined. They have a wedge shaped head, a medium-length muzzle with a definite stop, small pointed ears and an expressive face. The tail is tightly curled and, in profile, should be carried such that it is indistinguishable from the compact body of the dog.

Coat

Like all spitz, the Keeshonden have a dense double coat, with a thick ruff around the neck. Typically, the males of this breed will have a thicker, more pronounced ruff than the females. The tail is well plumed, and feathering on the fore and hind legs adds to the soft look of the breed. The coat is shown naturally, and should not be wavy, silky, or long enough to form a natural part down the back.

Color

The Keeshond is a color-specific spitz type; many of the names of the dog refer to the distinctive wolf color of the breed. The color is a mix of grey, black and cream. The top coat is tipped with black, while the undercoat is silver or cream (never tawny). The color can range from very pale to very dark, but it should neither be black nor white, and the ruff and "trousers" of the hind legs should be a distinctly lighter silver or cream.

The plumed tail should be of a silver or cream color with a black tip on the very end. The tail should be tightly curled over the back. The tail is an important part of the Keeshond's shape. The ears and muzzle are to be black, although some tend to develop "milk mouth" or a white shading around the nose and front of the muzzle. This increases as the dog ages. In American shows, this white shading is acceptable, although not desired.

It is also important to note that the feet are to also be of the same cream, or lighter grey color as the legs. Feet that are totally black or white are not allowed. However, light pencilling is accepted.

The other important marking is the "spectacles," a delicate dark line running from the outer corner of each eye toward the lower corner of each ear, which, coupled with markings forming short eyebrows, is necessary for the distinct expressive look of the breed. All markings should be clear, not muddled or broken. Absence of the spectacles is considered a serious fault. The eyes should be dark brown, almond-shaped with black eye rims.

Ears should be small, triangular, and erect.

Temperament

Keeshonden tend to be very playful, with quick reflexes and strong jumping ability. They are quick learners and eager to please. Because Keeshonden are quick learners, they also learn the things you didn't necessarily wish to teach them - very quickly. However, Keeshonden make excellent agility and obedience dogs. So amenable to proper training is this bright, sturdy dog that Keeshonden have been successfully trained to serve as guide dogs for the blind; only their lack of size has prevented them from being more widely used in this role.

They love children and are excellent family dogs, preferring to be close to their humans whenever possible. They generally get along with other dogs as well and will enjoy a good chase around the yard. Keeshonden are very intuitive and empathic and are often used as comfort dogs. Most notably, at least one Keeshond, Tikva, was at Ground Zero on 9/11 to help comfort the rescue workers. The breed has a tendency to become especially clingy towards their owners, even in comparison to other dogs. If their owner is out, or in another room behind a closed door, they may sit, waiting for their owner to reappear, even if there are other people nearby. Many have been referred to as their "owner's shadow," or "velcro dogs".

They are known by their loud distinctive bark. Throughout the centuries, the Keeshond has been very popular as a watch dog on manors in the Netherlands and middle Europe; this trait is evident to this day, and they are alert dogs that warn their owners of any new visitors. Despite being a loud and alert watch dog, Keeshonden are not aggressive towards visitors. They generally welcome visitors affectionately once their family has accepted them. Unfortunately, barking may become a problem if not properly handled. Keeshonden that are kept in a yard and not allowed to be with their humans are unhappy, and often become nuisance barkers.

Training

The Keeshond is a very bright dog as evidenced by its level of achievement in obedience work. The Keeshond ranks 16th in Stanley Coren's The Intelligence of Dogs, being of excellent working/obedience intelligence. This intelligence makes a Keeshond a good choice for the dog owner who is willing to help a dog learn the right lessons, but also entails added responsibility.

Many people purchase a Keeshond thinking that, since they are agreeable family dogs, they must also be easy to train. While affectionate, Keeshonden may not be for the inexperienced trainer. Consistency and fairness are needed and, while most dogs need a structured environment, it is especially necessary with a Keeshond. Like most of the independent-minded spitz breeds, Keeshonden respond poorly to heavy-handed or forceful training methods.

Many behavioral problems with Keeshonden stem from these intelligent dogs inventing their own activities (often destructive ones, like digging and chewing) out of boredom. They need daily contact with their owners and lots of activity to remain happy. Therefore, it is not the right choice of breed for those who want a dog that lives happily alone in a kennel or backyard.

Keeshonden can also be timid dogs. It is important to train them to respect their owners and family, but not fear them. Keeshonden want to please their owners, so harsh punishment is not necessary when the dog does not obey as quickly as desired. They like to spend time with their owners, and love attention.

Health

Keeshonden are generally a very healthy breed. Though congenital health issues are not common, the conditions which have been known to sometimes occur in Keeshonden are hip dysplasia, luxating patellas (trick knee), epilepsy, Cushing's disease, primary hyperparathyroidism, and hypothyroidism. Von Willebrand's disease has been known in Keeshonden but is very rare. An accurate test for the gene causing primary hyperparathyroidism [1] (or PHPT) has recently been developed at Cornell University. As with any breed, it is important when buying a puppy to make sure that the parents have been tested and certified free from inherited problems. A healthy, well-bred Keeshond can be expected to live between 12 and 15 years on average.

Grooming

Due to their double coat, a thick undercoat and a longer "guard" coat above that, Keeshonden need regular brushing. An hour per week will keep the dog comfortable and handsome. The Keeshond's coat sheds dirt when dry, and the breed is not prone to doggy odor, so only infrequent bathing is necessary. The coat acts as insulation and protects the dog from sunburn and insects, so shaving or clipping is not desirable. The coat also loses its distinct color as the black tipping on the hairs will be shorn off. If frequent brushing is too much effort, it is better to choose another breed rather than clip the Keeshond short.

History

The Keeshond was named after the 18th-century Dutch Patriot, Cornelis (Kees) de Gyselaer (spelled 'Gijselaar' in Modern Dutch), leader of the rebellion against the House of Orange. The dog became the rebels' symbol, and when the House of Orange returned to power, this breed almost disappeared. The word 'keeshond' is a compound word: 'Kees' is a nickname for Cornelius (de Gyselaer), and 'hond' is the Dutch word for dog. In the Netherlands, "keeshond" is the term for German Spitzes that encompass them all from the toy or dwarf (Pomeranian) to the Wolfsspitz (Keeshond). The sole difference between the German Spitzes is their coloring and size guidelines. Although many American references point to the Keeshond as we know it originating in the Netherlands, the breed is cited as being part of the German Spitz family and originating in Germany along with the Pomeranian (toy or dwarf German Spitz) and American Eskimo dog (small or standard German Spitz) according to the FCI.

The first standard for "Wolfsspitze" was posted at the Dog Show of 1880 in Berlin. The Club for German Spitzes was founded in 1899. The German standard was revised in 1901 to specify the characteristic color that we know today, "silver grey tipped with black". In the late 1800s the "Overweight Pomeranian", a white German Spitz and most likely a Standard German Spitz, was shown in the British Kennel Club. The "Overweight Pomeranian" was no longer recognized by the British Kennel Club in 1915. In the 1920s, Baroness van Hardenbroeck took an interest in the breed and began to build it up again. The Nederlandse Keeshond Club was formed in 1924. The Dutch Barge Dog Club of England was formed in 1925 by Mrs. Wingfield-Digby and accepted into the British Kennel Club in 1926, when the breed and the club were renamed to Keeshond.

Carl Hinderer is credited with bringing his Schloss Adelsburg Kennel, which he founded in 1922 in Germany, with him to America in 1923. His German Champion Wolfsspitz followed him two by two in 1926. As in England, Germany was not regarded fondly in America at the time and the Wolfsspitz/Keeshond was not recognized by the AKC. Despite this, Carl joined the Maryland KC and attended local shows. Due to the lack of AKC recognition Carl had to register each puppy with his club in Germany.

Carl regularly wrote to the AKC including the New York headquarters to promote the Wolfsspitz. While going through New York on his way to Germany in 1930 Carl visited the AKC offices and presented Wachter, his Germany champion, to AKC president, Dr. DeMond, who promptly agreed to start the recognition process, with some caveats including changing the name to Keeshond, and asked Carl to bring back all the relevant data from Germany. Carl also translated the German standard to English for the AKC. The Keeshond was accepted for AKC registration in 1930.

Despite intense lobbying the FCI would not accept the Keeshond as a separate breed since it viewed the Wolfsspitz and Keeshond as identical. In 1997 the German Spitz Club updated its standard so that the typically smaller Keeshond preferred in America and other English-speaking countries could be included. This greatly expanded the gene pool and unified the standard internationally for the first time. Now bred for many generations as a companion dog, the Keeshond easily becomes a loving family member.

As a result of the breed's history and friendly disposition, Keeshonden are sometimes referred to as "The Smiling Dutchman".

Miscellaneous

Breed pronunciation

Out of the 350 some purebreds, the Keeshond has possibly the most mispronounced name. "Kay sawn", "Case-hond", "kās-hond", "keys-hând", "keesh-ond", "keesh-hond", and even "keesh-hound" as so many will say, are all improper pronunciations . The proper pronunciation is "kayz-hond" or "kayz-hawnd" with the proper pronunciation of the plural being "kayz-honden" or "kayz-hawnden" .

Colored Keeshonden

Historically, Keeshonden being part of the German Spitz family had been interbred with their smaller brethren (small, standard, and dwarf German spitzes) and came in several colors—white, black, red, orange, orange-shaded white (also called orange and cream), and silver gray. Originally, like the other German spitzes, many colors, including piebalds, were allowed, but as time progressed, only the silver-grey and cream (wolf-gray) color was finally established into the Wolfsspitz type. [2]

While other-colored Keeshonden can have terrific conformation, they're not allowed to be shown in the show ring. Colored Keeshonden are considered "pet quality" and thus should be spayed or neutered.

The appearance of oddly-colored Kees in otherwise wolf-gray litters has caused research into the early history of Keeshond coat colors. Because of this, some breeders wonder whether the Keeshond should be bred for colors other than grey. There are many bloodlines carrying the colored gene, and rather than examples of mixed breeding, colors are legitimate throwbacks to an earlier era of the breed.

No one knows the exact number of colored Keeshonden born in the United States. Incorrect or incomplete documentation make it impossible to determine how many colored Keeshonden, and of which colors, have been born in the United States.

External links

- Clubs, Associations, and Societies
  - Keeshond Club of America [3]
  - Keeshond Club of Canada [4]
  - Keeshond Club UK [5]
  - Keeshond Club of Sweden [6]
  - Keeshond Rescue of North America [7]
  - Verein für Deutsche Spitze (Club for German Spitzes) [8]
  - Keeshond Club of Finland [9]
- Pedigree Database
  - Keeshond Pedigree and Health Database [10]
  - Keeshond Pedigree (and Health coming soon) Database 61000+ records [11]

Lhasa Apso

The **Lhasa Apso** ( ) (most properly spelled Lhasa apso) is a non-sporting dog breed originating in Tibet. It was bred as an interior sentinel in the Buddhist monasteries, who alerted the monks to any intruders who entered. Lhasa is the capital city of Tibet and *apso* is a word in the Tibetan language meaning "bearded," so *Lhasa Apso* simply means "long-haired Tibetan dog."

Male Lhasa Apsos should ideally be 10.75 inches at the withers and weigh about 14-18 pounds, 6–8 kg. The females are slightly smaller, and weigh between 12-14 pounds, 5–7 kg. The breed standard requires dark brown eyes and a black nose, although liver coloured lhasas have a brown nose. The texture of the coat is heavy, straight, hard, neither woolly nor silky, and very dense. Colors include Black, white, golden, rust and parti-colored with various shadings. Lhasas can be with or without dark tips at the end of ears and beard. The tail should be carried well over the dog's back. The breed standard currently used by the American Kennel Club was approved on July 11, 1978. Lhasas can change color as they get older, starting with a dark brown coat which gradually turns lighter.

Temperament

Having been bred as an indoor monastery sentinel dog by Tibetan Buddhist monks, Lhasa Apsos are alert with a keen sense of hearing with a rich, sonorous bark that belies their size. The ideal Lhasa temperament is to be wary of strangers while being loyal to those closest to them. They can be very aggressive to strangers untrained. They rank 68th in Stanley Coren's The Intelligence of Dogs, being of fair working/obedience intelligence. Lhasa Apsos are independent as well as companion dogs who want to please their owners. Unique personality characteristics of Lhasa Apsos have gained them a reputation as being a very emotive breed that in some cases prove themselves to be completely fearless. Lhasa Apsos often show happiness by rubbing their head on their owners, running and rolling around, or sitting on their owner's feet.

A Lhasa Apso responds to exercise and discipline with a calm assertive energy. These dogs require socialization with dogs and other people early as puppies and throughout their lives. They require patience but in return can be quite comical, entertaining and caring companions. They aim to please their owners and enjoy training. While their personality belies their size, they need a home that is mindful that there is a small dog in the house to prevent injury. They enjoy vantage points in the house where they can view all that is going on.

If properly trained early as a puppy, the Lhasa Apso will come to appreciate bathing, hair combing and clipping, but they generally do not enjoy bathing or swimming as this is not part of their breed traits.

The Lhasa Apso is a long-lived breed, with some living in good health into their early 20s. There are few health problems specific to the breed. Their vision may deteriorate with age but they are not sight-oriented dogs and they endure blindness with few noticeable changes in behavior.

History

The Lhasa Apso originated in Tibet, perhaps as long ago as 800 B.C., which makes it one of the oldest recognized breeds in the world. Recent research* has shown the Lhasa as one of the breeds most closely related to the ancestral wolf. (Others are Akita, Shiba Inu, Shar-Pei, Chow, Basenji, Alaskan Malamute, Siberian Husky, Saluki, Afghan, Pekingese, Shih Tzu, and Samoyed.)

Referred to in Tibet as Apso Seng Kyi, best translated as "Bearded Lion Dog," the Lhasa's primary function was that of a household sentinel, guarding the homes of Tibetan nobility and Buddhist monasteries, particularly in or near the sacred city of Lhasa. The large Tibetan Mastiffs guarded the monasteries' entrances, but the keen hearing and sharp bark of the Lhasa Apso served to warn residents if an intruder happened to get past the exterior guards. These little guardians were highly prized. It was believed that the bodies of the Lhasa Apsos could be entered by souls of deceased lamas while they awaited reincarnation into a new body. Lhasas in Tibet were never sold. The only way a person could get one was as a gift.

The Lhasa Apso originated in Tibet, where they were bred as sentinels for palaces and monasteries. In the early 1900s, a few of the breed were brought by military men returning from the Indian subcontinent to England, where the breed was referred to as "Lhasa Terriers". Lhasa Apsos would alert outdoor dogs, such as the Tibetan Mastiff, of any danger they perceived their owners, Tibetan Lamas, may be in with their keen sense of hearing and deep bark. In this sense, Lhasa Apsos are used to working with larger dogs and may relate to them more than small "yappy" dogs.

The original American pair of Lhasas was a gift from Thubten Gyatso, 13th Dalai Lama to C. Suydam Cutting, arriving in the United States in 1933. Mr. Cutting had traveled in Tibet and met the Dalai Lama there. At this time, there was only one Lhasa Apso registered in England. The breed was called first the Apso Lhasa Terrier, then the Lhasa Apso. The American Kennel Club officially accepted the breed in 1935 in the Terrier Group, and in 1959 transferred the breed to the Non-Sporting Group. In the UK, they are placed in the Utility Group. Certain characteristics which are part of the breed type evolved as a result of geographical and climatic environment - the high altitudes, the dry windy climate, the dusty terrain, the short hot summer and the long bitterly cold winter of the Himalaya region. Among these are head features, the coat, eye-fall, the musculation and body structure, the general hardness and longevity of the breed.

Recently, DNA Analysis has identified the Lhasa Apso as one of the 14 most ancient dog breeds, verifying that lap dogs and companion dogs were among the first dogs bred by humans. "

Currently, there is worldwide concern that it is necessary to breed some of the original Tibetan Lhasa Apsos into the Western bred line which is now 60-years old, to maintain the Tibetan authenticity of the breed. The two lines now differ in some ways which is a concern to breeders who want to properly preserve the breed.

Shedding

Like most mammals, all dogs slough off dander. Since dander and many other allergens become trapped in hair, and shed hairs are light enough to spend considerable time airborne indoors before settling to the floor to be removed during housecleaning (an activity which can, ironically, help them stay airborne), shedding of the coat is a typical way in which house-pets spread their allergens in a domestic environment.

Coming from the extremely cold weather of the Himalayas, the Apso has a double coat: only the undercoat, which is soft, will shed out once a year, the outer coat, consisting of coarse outer guard hairs, does not shed. Many owners do not show their dogs's full coat and tend to keep their Lhasa Apsos in a "puppy clip." People with allergies can co-exist with the low-shedding breeds of dogs, including the Lhasa Apso, when they are properly cared for.

Health

The lhasa apso is known to suffer from a few health problems. For example, it is known to suffer from Sebaceous Adenitis - a hereditary skin disease that occurs primarily in Standard Poodles, but has also been reported in a number of other breeds, including the Lhasa Apso. They are also known to suffer from the genetic disease Progressive Retinal Atrophy which can render them blind. Ethical, responsible breeders will have their breeding dogs checked yearly (CERF'd) by a canine ophthalmologist to check that they are not developing the disease, which is heritable in offspring.

Miscellaneous

- The Brazilian comic series Monica's Gang features a green-colored Lhasa Apso named Fluffy which belongs to Jimmy Five.
- In the animated series Spider-Man and his Amazing Friends, Peter's Aunt May owns a lhasa apso named Ms. Lion.
- Lhasa Apso has also appeared in at least one episode of the Simpsons. In the episode Three Gays of the Condo, Homer Simpson moved in with a couple of gay men. Homer started to act like a gay man and got a Lhasa Apso. Also, Milhouse Van Houten owns a lhasa apso.
- In "The L Word", Helena is assured by her wealthy mother that she was going to leave her inheritance to her, not to her Lhasa Apsos.
- Lhasa Apso are said to bring luck, hence the saying "Lucky Lhasa".".
- Singer Arturo Paz owns a Lhasa Apso named Coco, seen on Tiger Beat.
- Actress/Singer-Songwriter Keke Palmer has a Lhasa Apso named Rusty, seen in a picture on MTV Cribs.
- A Lhasa Apso is both a major character and a plot device in the Newbery Award-winning 1948 children's novel, *Daughter of the Mountains,* by Louise Rankin (ISBN 978-0140363357).

- Singer Gwen Stefani had a Lhasa Apso dog called Lamb/Meggan.
- A Lhasa appears in Disney's animated feature film Lady and the Tramp as the pound dog Peg.

External links

- American Lhasa Apso Club [1]
- Kai-La-Sha [2]
- Lhasa Apso information and Genetics [3]
- Lhasa Apso Rescue [4]
- Lhasa Apso pictures and articles [5]
- Gompa Lhasa Apso Preservation Program & Trust [6]

Löwchen

The **Löwchen** (German: "little lion") is breed of dog that once had the dubious distinction, like the Portuguese Water Dog and the Havanese, of being the rarest dog in the world. Even today, the breed generally has fewer than a few hundred new registrations each year worldwide.

Description

Appearance

The Löwchen is, depending on the source, bichon type dog, with a long, silky coat that is presented in a lion cut for conformation show purposes. This means that the haunches, back legs, front legs (except bracelets around the ankles), and the 1/3 of the tail closest to the body are shaved, and the rest of the coat is left natural to give the appearance of a lion-like form. A small dog, they are considered by some registries as toy dog, and have been long-time companions of royal courts.

The head of the Löwchen is one of the most important features, with its short, wide muzzle, broad skull, lively round eyes, and pendulant ears. The head, when in proportion to the body, is neither too big nor too small, but helps to emphasize the friendly, regal, and leonine personality of the Löwchen.

The coat should not be thin and fluffy like a Bichon Frise, but wavy with a mix of thicker hairs amongst the fine ones. This allows for a flowing coat that is not frizzy or fly-away, and a Löwchen coat should neither be soft like a nor harsh like many terriers. They can come in all colours, including brown, that allow for dark eyes and nose.

Temperament

The Löwchen is a friendly, happy dog. Dogs of this breed are both active and playful, and very intelligent. The Löwchen makes a good pet for families with children and an excellent house pet.

History

Although this dog may be related to the Bichon Frise, the Löwchen's history remains obscure. The little 'lion dog' is seen in many art pieces featuring dogs as far back as the 1500s, but it is unclear whether these were all dogs like the Löwchen, or simply small dogs of the Bichon type that were trimmed in a lion cut.

It is an old breed type, found in many countries as far back as the 1500s. The modern sources of the breed were from Belgium, France and Germany enthusiasts in the late 19th century.

External links

- Löwchen Club of Canada [1]
- Löwchen Club UK [2]
- Löwchen Club of America [3]
- / Löwchen & Lhasa Apso Exclusive Show Dogs [4]

Poodle

For the political insult see poodle (insult).

The **poodle** is a breed of dog, and is regarded as the second most intelligent breed of dog after the border collie, and before the German Shepherd. The poodle breed is found officially in toy, miniature, and standard sizes, with many coat colors. Originally bred as a type of water dog, the poodle is skillful in many dog sports, including agility, obedience, tracking, and even herding. Poodles are elegant in the conformation ring, having taken top honors in many shows, including "Best in Show" at the Westminster Kennel Club Dog Show in 1991 and 2002, and at the World Dog Show in 2007.

History

Poodles are retrievers or gun dogs, and can still be seen in that role. The poodle is believed to have originated in Germany, where it is known as the Pudel. The English word "poodle" comes from the Low German *pudel* or *puddeln* , meaning to splash in the water. The breed was standardized in France, where it was commonly used as a water retriever.

The American Kennel Club states that the large, or Standard, Poodle is the oldest of the three varieties and that the dog gained special fame as a water worker. So widely was it used as retriever that it was bred with a moisture-resistant coat to further facilitate progress in swimming. Thence came the custom of clipping to pattern which so enhanced the style and general appearance that its sponsors, particularly in France, were captivated by it. All of the Poodle's ancestors were acknowledged to be good swimmers, although one member of the family, the truffle dog (which may have been of Toy or Miniature size), it is said, never went near the water. Truffle hunting was widely practiced in England, and later in Spain and Germany, where the edible fungus has always been considered a delicacy. For scenting and digging up the fungus, the smaller dogs were favored, since they did less damage to the truffles with their feet than the larger kinds. So it is rumored that a terrier was crossed with the Poodle to produce the ideal truffle hunter.

Despite the standard poodle's claim to greater age than the other varieties, there is some evidence to show that the smaller types developed only a short time after the breed assumed the general type by which it is recognized today. The smallest, or Toy variety, was developed in England in the 18th century, when the White Cuban became popular there. This was a sleeve dog attributed to the West Indies from whence it traveled to Spain and then to England. The continent had known the poodle long before it came to England. Drawings by the German artist, Albrecht Durer, establish the breed in the 15th and 16th centuries. It was the principal pet dog of the later 18th century in Spain, as shown by the paintings of the Spanish artist Francisco Goya. France had toy poodles as pampered favorites during the reign of Louis XVI at about the same period.

Characteristics

Appearance

Most poodles have a dense, curly, non-sheddingcoat that requires regular grooming. Since poodles do not have the plush double coat of many breeds, their fur is often referred to as "hair", a term usually reserved for humans. Most poodles are solid-colored, and many registries allow only solid colors in conformation shows. "Parti" (short for parti-colored) poodles have large patches of colors different from the main body color. "Phantom" poodles have the color pattern of a black-and-tan dog, although not necessarily black and tan. Solid-colored poodles may either "hold" their color (i.e., stay more or less the same throughout their lives) or "fade" or "clear" to a lighter shade. Usually the ears and the thicker guard hairs hold more of the original color than other hair.

The tail is usually poofy, often docked in the US and less often in Europe; the practice is illegal in the UK and Australia. Tails, when docked, are left much longer than in the past. "Bunny-like tails" (very short-docked tails) are now rarely seen except among puppy mill pet shop dogs. Poodles have drop ears which are never cropped.

Poodle sizes

Unlike many breeds, poodles can come in a variety of sizes, distinguished by adult shoulder (withers) height. The exact height cutoffs among the varieties vary slightly from country to country. Non-Fédération Cynologique Internationale kennel clubs generally recognize three sizes, *standard*, *miniature*, and *toy*, sometimes as sizes of the same breed, and sometimes as separate breeds. The Fédération Cynologique Internationale recognizes four sizes of one breed, *standard*, *medium*, *miniature*, and *toy*. Only the Fédération Cynologique Internationale describes a maximum size for standard poodles. France is the country responsible for the breed in the Fédération Cynologique Internationale, and in this country the puppies of all sizes are listed together.. The terms *royal standard*, *teacup*, and *tiny teacup* are marketing names, and are not recognized by any major kennel club.

Comparison of poodle sizes defined by major kennel clubs

Size	The Kennel Club (UK)	Australian National Kennel Council	New Zealand Kennel Club	Canadian Kennel Club	American Kennel Club	United Kennel Club	Fédération Cynologique Internationale
Standard, Grande	over 38 cm (15 ins)	38 cm (15 ins) and over	38 cm (15 ins) and over	over 15 inches (38 cm)	over 15 inches (38 cm)	over 15 inches (38 cm)	over 45 cm to 60 cm (+2 cm) (18ins to 24ins)
Medium, Moyen	not used	not used	not used	not used	not used	not used	over 35 cm to 45 cm (14ins to 18ins)
Miniature - Dwarf, Nain	28 cm to 38 cm (11ins to 15ins)	28 cm to under 38 cm (11ins to 15ins)	28 cm to under 38 cm (11ins to 15ins)	over 10ins to under 15ins (25.4 cm to 38 cm)	over 10ins to 15ins (25.4 cm to 38 cm)	over 10ins up to 15ins (25.4 cm to 38 cm)	over 28 cm to 35 cm (11ins to 14ins)
Toy	under 28 cm (11 ins)	under 28 cm (11 ins)	under 28 cm (11 ins)	under 10ins (25.4 cm)	under 10ins (25.4 cm)	under 10ins (25.4 cm)	24 cm to 28 cm (9.4ins to 11ins)

All the Fédération Cynologique Internationale poodles are in Group 9 *Companion and Toy*, Section 2 *Poodle*. All the Kennel Club poodles are in the Utility Group. All three sizes of poodle for the Australian National Kennel Council and the New Zealand Kennel Club are in the Non-Sporting Group. The Canadian Kennel Club and the American Kennel Club place standard and miniature sizes in the Non-Sporting Group, and the toy size in the Toy Group. The United Kennel Club places the miniature and toy in the Companion Group and the standard poodle in the Gundog Group.

Coat

Unlike most dogs which have double coats, poodles have a single layer (no undercoat) of dense, curly fur that sheds minimally and could be considered hypoallergenic (though not completely allergen free). Texture ranges from coarse and woolly to soft and wavy. Poodle show clips require many hours of brushing and care per week, about 10 hours/week for a standard poodle. Poodles are usually clipped down as soon as their show career is over and put into a lower-maintenance cut. Pet clips are much less elaborate than show and require much less maintenance. A pet owner can anticipate grooming a poodle every six to eight weeks. Although professional grooming is often costly, poodles are easy to groom at home with the proper equipment.

Show clips

Many breed registries allow only certain clips for poodles shown in conformation. In American Kennel Club shows, adults must be shown in the "Continental" or "English saddle" clips. Dogs under 12 months old may be shown with a "puppy clip." The United Kennel Club (US) allows in addition a *Sporting Clip*, similar to the puppy clip, with the fur trimmed short for hunting dogs. The American Kennel Club allows the Sporting Clip in Stud Dog and Brood Bitch classes as well.

Some sources believe the show clips evolved from working clips, which originally provided warmth to major joints when the dogs were immersed in cold water. The rest of the body is shaved for less drag in the water. Others express skepticism at this theory, instead citing the French circus as the origin of the entertaining and unique clips.

Second Puppy

This clip is also called the Scandinavian clip or puppy clip. It was invented by Swedish and Norwegian show groomers in the 1970s. This clip is the most common one in all sizes for shows in Europe, and is allowed for adult poodles to be shown in the FCI countries. The face, throat, belly, feet and the base of the tail are shaved 5 to 7 days before the show to get a nice smooth appearance of the shaved areas. The hair on the head is left to form a "topknot" that is fixed by using latex bands; in most European countries, hair spray is banned. The rest of the dog is shaped with scissors. It makes the parts of the dog look fluffy.

Continental clip

In the continental clip the face, throat, feet and part of the tail are shaved. The upper half of the front legs is shaved, leaving "fluffy pompons" around the ankles. The hindquarters are shaved except for pompons on the lower leg (from the hock to the base of the foot) and optional round areas (sometimes called "rosettes") over the hips. The continental clip is the most popular show clip today.

English Saddle clip

The English saddle clip is similar to the continental, except for the hindquarters. The hindquarters are not shaved except a small curved area on each flank (just behind the body), the feet, and bands just below the stifle (knee) and above the hock, leaving three pompons. This clip is now rarely seen in standard poodles.

Pet clips

Pet clips can be simple or as elaborate as owners wish. The hair under the tail should always be kept short to keep feces from matting in the poodle's curls. Most owners also keep the feet and face clipped short to prevent dirt from matting between toes and food from matting around the dog's muzzle. Beyond these sanitary requirements, desired clips depend on owners' preferences. Some owners maintain a longer clip in winter than summer, which they groom often with a wire slicker brush to remove tangles and prevent matting.

Corded coat

In most cases, whether a poodle is in a pet or show clip, hair is completely brushed out. Poodle hair can also be "corded" with rope-like mats similar to those of a Komondor or human dreadlocks. Though once as common as the curly poodle, corded poodles are now rare. Corded coats are difficult to keep clean and take a long time to dry after washing. Any poodle with a normal coat can be corded when their adult coat is in. Corded poodles may be shown in all major kennel club shows.

Temperament

Otherwise notable is this breed's keen sense for instinctual behavior. In particular, marking and hunting drives are more readily observable than in most other breeds. Even Toys will point birds. Classified as highly energetic, poodles can also get bored fairly easily and have been known to get creative about finding mischief. Poodles like to be in the center of things and are easily trained to do astonishing tricks involving both brains and agility. They have performed in circuses for centuries, beginning in Europe, and have been part of the Ringling Circus in its various forms from its inception. The Grimaldis, the famous British clowns Kenneth and Audrey Austin, "developed a stronger circus act" with a clever poodle named 'Twinkle,' the success of which allowed them to continue performing even as octogenarians."

Poodles are extremely people-oriented dogs and generally eager to please. Standard poodles in particular tend to be good with children. Poodles are adaptable and easy to train. Like most dogs, they appreciate daily exercise, such as a walk or a play session. Most are fairly agile and athletic.

Toy poodles will play ball and love to fetch. Play time is vital, but one must be sure that they get plenty of rest following long play periods and that fresh water is available at all times.

Poodles are very easy to housebreak. Whether going outside or being trained on a pad, they learn quickly where to defecate. They are still animals, however, and they need time to understand what is desired of them. It may take a while, but poodles are quite smart and learn more quickly than most dogs.

Health

The most common serious health issues of standard poodles (listed in order of the number of reported cases in the Poodle Health Registry [1] (as of August 20, 2007) are Addison's disease, gastric dilatation volvulus (GDV = bloat/torsion), thyroid issues (hyperthyroid and hypothyroid), tracheal collapse, epilepsy, sebaceous adenitis, juvenile renal disease, hip dysplasia, and cancer. Standard poodles are also susceptible to some health issues usually too minor to report to the poodle health registry. The most common of these minor issues are probably ear infections. Ear infections are a problem in all poodle varieties. Ear problems can be minimized by proper ear care. A veterinarian should be consulted if the dog shows signs of an ear infection.

Addison's Disease

Addison's disease is (as of August 20, 2007) the illness most commonly reported to the Poodle Health Registry. The number of reported cases of Addison's disease is nearly twice as high as the next most common problem (GDV). Addison's disease is characterized by insufficient production of glucocorticoid and/or mineralocortoid in the adrenal cortex. Addison's is often undiagnosed because early symptoms are vague and easily mistaken for other conditions. Standard poodles with unexplained lethargy, frequent gastric disturbances, or an inability to tolerate stress should be tested for Addison's. Addison's can cause fatal sodium/potassium imbalances, but, if caught early and treated with lifelong medication, most dogs can live a relatively normal life.

Gastric dilatation volvulus

Standard poodle owners should take special note of the high incidence of GDV in this breed. Excess gas trapped in the dog's stomach causes "bloat." Twisting of the stomach (volvulus or "torsion") causes or is caused by excess gas. Symptoms include restlessness, inability to get comfortable, pacing, or retching without being able to bring up anything. The dog's abdomen may be visibly swollen, but dogs can bloat or torsion without visible swelling. GDV is a dire emergency condition. If you suspect a dog is bloating, you should not wait to see if he improves. A dog with GDV requires immediate veterinary care. The dog's survival usually depends on whether the owner can get him to the vet in time. It is a good idea for a standard poodle owner to know the route to the nearest 24-hour emergency clinic, so time is not wasted looking for directions.

Longevity and causes of death

Standard poodles in UK, Denmark and USA/Canada surveys had a median lifespan of 11.5 to 12 years. In a UK survey, the most common causes of death were cancer (30%), old age (18%), GDV (bloat/torsion, 6%), and cardiac disease (5%).

Miniature and toy poodles in UK surveys had median lifespans of 14 to 14.5 years. In miniature poodles, the leading cause of death was old age (39%). In toy poodles, the leading causes of death were old age (25%) and kidney failure (20%).

Some toy poodles can live up to 20 years, if they have a healthy life and are not overweight.

Common illnesses

- Addison's disease (hypoadrenocorticism)
- Cataracts
- Congenital heart disease
- Chronic active hepatitis
- Cushing's syndrome (hyperadrenocorticism)
- Distichiasis
- Entropion
- Epilepsy
- Gastric dilatation volvulus (Standard)
- Gastric torsion
- Glaucoma
- Intervertebral disc degeneration
- Lacrimal duct atresia
- Legg–Calvé–Perthes syndrome
- Progressive retinal atrophy
- Patellar luxation (Toy and Miniature)
- Trichiasis
- Urolithiasis.
- Hip dysplasia (Standard)
- Hypothyroidism
- Mitral valve disease
- Osteosarcoma
- Patent ductus arteriosus
- Sebaceous adenitis
- Von Willebrand disease

Poodle mixes

Poodles are crossed with other breeds for various reasons, and the resulting puppies (called designer dogs) are described by whimsical portmanteau words, such as cockapoo or spoodle (Cocker Spaniel cross), goldendoodle, labradoodle (Labrador cross), pekepoos (Pekingese cross), and many others.

A cross between a shedding breed and a poodle (which doesn't shed much) does not reliably produce a non-shedding dog. Traits of puppies from crossbreedings are not as predictable as those from purebred poodle breedings, and the crosses may shed or have unexpected or undesirable qualities from the parent breeds.

Poodle crossbreds (also called *hybrids*) are not recognized by any major breed registry, as crossbreeds are not one breed of dog, but two. If both parents are registered purebreds but of different breeds, it is still not possible to register a puppy as two different breeds. Some minor registries and Internet registry businesses will register dogs as any breed the owner chooses with minimal or no documentation; some even allow the breeder or owner to make up a new "breed name" (portmanteau word).

Hypoallergenic qualities

Poodles are often cited as a hypoallergenic dog breed. The poodle's individual hair follicles have an active growth period that is longer than that of many other breeds of dogs; combined with the tightly curled coat, which slows the loss of dander and dead hair by trapping it in the curls, an individual poodle may release less dander and hair into the environment. In addition, most poodles are frequently brushed and bathed to keep them looking their best; this not only removes hair and dander but also controls the other potent allergen, saliva.

Although hair, dander, and saliva can be minimized, they are still present and can stick to "clothes and the carpets and furnishings in your home"; inhaling them, or being licked by the dog, can trigger a reaction in a sensitive person. A vacuum cleaner with a HEPA filter can help clear dander floating in the air.

The word hypoallergenic, when referring to a dog, is also a misconception; all dogs shed. Poodles shed hair in minimal amounts, and also release dander, but are not as likely to trigger allergies as much as many other breeds.

Famous poodles

- Aero, Mao Asada's pet.
- Aida, pet of ice hockey player Žigmund Pálffy.
- Algonquin from *Elvira, Mistress of the Dark*.
- Atman and Butz, Schopenhauer's pets.
- Basket, Basket II, and Basket III, successive pets of Gertrude Stein and Alice B. Toklas.
- Bela, "Weird Al" Yankovic's poodle who sat on his head for the cover of his 2003 album Poodle Hat.
- Maui and Blondie, Ashley Tisdale's toy poodle and Maltipoo
- Shadow, Vanessa Hudgens' toy poodle
- Boy, pet of Prince Rupert of the Rhine (1619-1682) and killed at the Battle of Marston Moor.
- Charley, pet of Nobel Prize-winning author John Steinbeck, a black (referred to as "blue" in the book) standard poodle played Charley in the TV miniseries "Travels with Charley: In Search of America," based on Steinbeck's 1961 book of the same name.
- Cleo, from *Clifford the Big Red Dog*.
- Derek, pet of Patrick Swayze
- Diswilliam and others, pets of Mary Tyler Moore
- Dusty Springfield, Joss Stone's pet.
- Fluffles from A Matter of Loaf and Death
- Georgette from Disney's "Oliver & Company."
- Gigi and Cash, pets of Christian Serratos.
- Jane Seymour third wife of Henry VIII had a pet white poodle, which even appears in the official portrait of Henry, Jane, and his parents, the previous King and Queen. She is said to have spent most of her time walking the poodle in the palace gardens or doing needlework.
- Josephine, prized pet of author Jacqueline Susann; subject of her first book, 1963's *Every Night, Josephine!*.
- Mephistopheles, incarnated in a poodle as described by Goethe in *Faust*.
- Mugatu, from the movie Zoolander, owned a white toy poodle.
- Puff, Suga Mama's pet poodle from *The Proud Family*.
- Poodle, a pet haruno in *Honey and Clover*
- Quiche Lorraine, Fred Schneider's surreal (dark green, strawberry blonde) pet poodle in The B-52's song "Quiche Lorraine".
- Roly, a poodle who was featured in the BBC's *EastEnders* for eight years.
- Rufus, pet of Winston Churchill
- Teddy, famous dog of radio talk show host Michael Savage.
- Vicky, pet of Richard and Pat Nixon.
- Wellington, famous macguffin from *The Curious Incident of the Dog in the Night-time,* by Mark Haddon.

- Yankee Poodle from *Captain Carrot and His Amazing Zoo Crew!*.
- Itchy and Scratchy, Chris Packham's poodles, see
- Bunyip, resident pooch in Australian TV soap 'The Secret Life of Us'

Notes

note 1. fur is defined by the Oxford English Dictionary as "the short, soft hair of certain animals" whereas hair is defined as "any of the fine thread-like strands growing from the skin of mammals and other animals, or from the epidermis of a plant."

External links

- Dog Breed Profile - Poodle [2]

Schipperke

A **Schipperke** (,) is a small Belgian breed of dog that originated in the early 16th century. There has been a long informal debate over whether this type of dog is a spitz or miniature sheepdog.

Description

Appearance and temperament

Their small, pointed ears are erect atop the head. Schipperkes are double coated with a soft, fluffy undercoat that is covered by a harsher-feeling and longer outer coat. One of the breed characteristics is a long ruff that surrounds the neck and then a strip trails down towards the rear of the dog. They also have a longer coat on their hind legs called culottes.

Dogs of this breed usually weigh between 3 and 9 kg (7 to 20 lb). Puppies are born with tails in different lengths, and in Canada and the United States, they are usually docked the day after birth. In countries that have bans on docking, Schipperkes display their natural tails which curve over the back of the dog (if the dog is happy and the tail is long enough).

Known for a stubborn, mischievous and headstrong temperament, the Schipperke is sometimes referred to as the "little black fox", the "Tasmanian black devil", or the "little black devil." They are naturally curious and high-energy dogs, and require ample exercise and supervision. Schipperkes are very smart and independent, and sometimes debate listening to owners, instead choosing to do whatever benefits them the most. First-time dog owners would be well-advised to familiarize themselves with the breed prior to purchase. Schipperkes require training and a secure, fenced-in space to run.They are formidable barkers and can be aggressive around other dogs.

Health

The Schipperke has no particular health problems, and individuals often reach the old age of 17 or 18 years. Nonetheless, inactivity, lack of exercise and over-feeding are very harmful, and can lead to joint and skeletal problems and tooth, heart, lung or digestive conditions.

The one caveat to the Schipperke's good health is MPS IIIB, a genetic mutation that occurs in at most 15% of the total breed population. The University of Pennsylvania School of Veterinary Medicine has developed a test for the disease and began accepting samples in April 2003.

Grooming

The Schipperke does not need expensive or excessive grooming. This breed is a moderate shedder, however. A brush that can reach the undercoat is the best. Regular weekly brushing is usually enough to keep the coat in good condition. There is no need for cutting or trimming and the ruff (hair around the neck) fluffs up naturally.

Schipperkes can "blow" their coats up to several times a year, and usually females more frequently than males. When this happens, they lose their undercoat. Owners typically find warm baths helpful during this time to remove the undercoat, rather than getting fur all over the home. Blowing their undercoat can last several days or weeks, and can take up to 2–3 months for schipperkes to grow back.

History

Schipperkes were first recognized as a formal breed in the 1880s, their standard being written in 1889. Much of what is known of their origins and early history comes from *Chasse et Pêche* (French for "Hunting and Fishing") magazine, articles of which were translated into English and published by the English magazine *The Stockkeeper*. The breed name of "Schipperke," officially taken in 1888, in English-speaking nations to mean "little boatman". In the 1920s, however, the people of Belgium decided they wanted the name to be a corruption of the Dutch word "Shapocke" or "Scheperke", meaning "little shepherd", because they noticed resemblance to the Belgium Sheepdog (Groenendael). This idea was first presented in an article in 1894 in the Chasse et Peche, where a Belgian man wrote, "if the little dog had not always been and was not still currently the watchdog of the boats from which he gets his name of "schipperke" (little boatman), you could have written "scheperke" (little shepherd)." It has been suggested that the idea of "little sailor" was an invention of the English, who mistook the Schipperke for a Dutch barge dog, this, however, has been disproved by the actual historical records. Some reports say they were found frequently as working dogs aboard barges in the canals, with three jobs onboard: security (barking vigorously when anyone approached the barge), keeping the barges free of vermin, and nipping at the towing horses' heels to get them moving to tow the barge. Due to their bravery and adventurous character, not to mention low center of gravity, Schipperkes are to this day known as excellent boat dogs, and are often found cruising the world aboard sailing yachts and powerboats. They are not prone to seasickness. Before the name "Schipperke" was officially taken, the breed was also known colloquially as "Spitzke". It is thought that the name change was to distinguish it from the German Spitz. Schipperkes are widely referred to in the U.S.A., albeit erroneously, as "Belgian barge dogs" or "Belgian ship dogs." It is often said that Schipperkes live up to their name. In World War II, the Belgian Resistance used the dogs to run messages between various resistance hideouts and cells, and the Nazis never caught on. Beatrix Potter, English author of the *Peter Rabbit* books, created a story called *The Pie and the Patty Pan* with a Schipperke named Duchess, who receives an invitation to tea. http://en.wikipedia.org/wiki/The_Tale_of_the_Pie_and_the_Patty-Pan

A Schipperke is also intermittently featured in the tiger-centric movie "Two Brothers." http://www.twobrothersmovie.net/

Similar breeds

As the Schipperke are a very ancient dog type, many smaller types of Spitz resemble each other. Medium to small sized breeds similar in appearance from various places in the world include the Wolfsspitz (Keeshond), Großspitz, Mittelspitz, Kleinspitz, Zwergspitz (Pomeranian), Samoyed (dog), Schipperke, Norwegian Elkhound, Volpino Italiano (Italian Spitz), Laika (Russian Spitz), Finnish Spitz, Indian Spitz, Japanese Spitz and the American Eskimo Dog.

External links

- Breed clubs
  - The Schipperke Club of America [1]
  - Schipperke Club of Belgium [2]
  - The Schipperke Club [3]
  - The Norwegian Schipperke Club [4]
- Information
  - Schipperke Health & Breed Information [5]
  - Schipperke Breed Information and Care Required [6]
  - Indepth Schipperke Dog Breed Information and Photos [7]
  - Information about the Schipperke [8]
  - General care and information about the Schipperke [9]
  - Le site Web du Schipperke [10]

Shiba Inu

The is the smallest of the six original and distinct breeds of dog from Japan.

A small, agile dog that copes very well with mountainous terrain, the Shiba Inu was originally bred for hunting. It is similar in appearance to the Akita, though much smaller in stature. It is one of the few ancient dog breeds still in existence in the world today.

Origin of the name

Inu is the Japanese word for dog, but the origin of the prefix "Shiba" is less clear. The word *shiba* means "brushwood" in Japanese, and refers to a type of tree or shrub whose leaves turn red in the fall. This leads some to believe that the Shiba was named with this in mind, either because the dogs were used to hunt in wild shrubs, or because the most common color of the Shiba Inu is a red color similar to that of the shrubs. However, in an old Nagano dialect, the word *shiba* also had the meaning of "small", thus this might be a reference to the dog's small size. Therefore, the Shiba Inu is sometimes translated as "Little Brushwood Dog".

Description

Appearance

The Shiba's frame is compact with well-developed muscles. Males and females are distinctly different in appearance: males are masculine without coarseness, females are feminine without weakness of structure. Males 14 1/2 inches to 16 1/2 inches (35–43 cm) at withers. Females 13 1/2 inches to 15 1/2 inches (33–41 cm). The preferred size is the middle of the range for each sex. Average weight at preferred size is approximately 23 pounds (10 kg) for males, 17 pounds (8 kg) for females. Bone is moderate.

Coat: Double coated with the outer coat being stiff and straight and the undercoat soft and thick. Fur is short and even on face, ears, and legs. Guard hairs stand off the body are about 1 1/2 to 2 inches in length at the withers. Tail hair is slightly longer and stands open in a brush. Shibas may be red, black and tan, or sesame (red with black-tipped hairs), with a cream, buff, or grey undercoat. They may also be cream, though this color is a major fault and should never be intentionally bred, as the required markings known as are not visible. "Urajiro" literally translates to "underside white". The *urajiro* (cream to white ventral color) is required in the following areas on all coat colors: on the sides of the muzzle, on the cheeks, inside the ears, on the underjaw and upper throat inside of legs, on the abdomen, around the vent and the ventral side of the tail. On reds: commonly on the throat, forechest, and chest. On blacks and sesames: commonly as a triangular mark on both sides of the forechest.

Temperament

Shiba Inus are generally independent and intelligent dogs. Some owners struggle with obedience training, but as with many dogs, socialization at a young age can greatly affect temperament. Traits such as independence and intelligence are often associated with ancient dog breeds, such as the Shiba Inu. Shibas should always be on a leash, unless in a secured area, because of their strong prey drive.

From the Japanese breed standard:

> A spirited boldness, a good nature, and an unaffected forthrightness, which together yield dignity and natural beauty. The Shiba has an independent nature and can be reserved toward strangers but is loyal and affectionate to those who earn his respect. They can be aggressive toward other dogs sometimes.

The terms , , and have subtle interpretations that have been the subject of much commentary.

The Shiba is a fastidious breed and feels the need to maintain itself in a clean state. They can often be seen licking their paws and legs much like a cat. They generally go out of their way to keep their coats clean, and while walking will avoid stepping in puddles, mud and dirt. Because of their fastidious and proud nature, the Shiba puppy is easy to housebreak and in many cases will housebreak themselves. Having their owner simply place them outside after meal times and naps is generally enough to teach the Shiba the appropriate method of toileting.

A distinguishing characteristic of the breed is the so-called "shiba scream". When sufficiently provoked or unhappy, the dog will produce a loud, high pitched scream. This can occur when attempting to handle the dog in a way that it deems unacceptable. The animal may also emit a very similar sound during periods of great joy, such as the return of the owner after an extended absence, or the arrival of a favored human guest.

History

Recent DNA analysis confirms that this is one of the oldest dog breeds, dating back to the 3rd century BC.

Originally, the Shiba Inu was bred to hunt and flush small game, such as birds and rabbits. Despite efforts to preserve the breed, the Shiba nearly became extinct during World War II due to a combination of bombing raids and a post-war distemper epidemic. All subsequent dogs were bred from the only three surviving bloodlines. These bloodlines were the Shinshu Shiba from Nagano Prefecture, the Mino Shiba from Gifu Prefecture, and the San'in Shiba from Tottori and Shimane Prefectures. The Shinshu Shibas possessed a solid undercoat, with dense layer of guard-hairs, and were small and red in color. The Mino Shibas tended to have thick, prick ears, and possessed a sickle tail, rather than the common curled tail found on most modern Shibas. The San'in Shibas were larger than most modern shibas, and tended to be black, without the common tan and white accents found on modern black-and-tan shibas. When the study of japanese dogs was formalized in the early and mid-twentieth century, these three strains were combined into one overall breed, the Shiba Inu. The first Japanese breed standard for the Shiba, the Nippo Standard, was published in 1934. In December 1936, the Shiba Inu was recognized as a Natural Monument of Japan through the Cultural Properties Act, largely due to the efforts of Nippo (Nihon Ken Hozonkai), the Association for the Preservation of the Japanese Dog.

In 1954, an armed service family brought the first Shiba Inu to the United States. In 1979, the first recorded litter was born in the United States. The Shiba was recognized by the American Kennel Club in 1992 and added to the AKC Non-Sporting Group in 1993. It is now primarily kept as a pet both in Japan and abroad.

Health

Health conditions known to affect this breed are glaucoma, cataracts, hip dysplasia, and luxating patella. Overall, however, they are of great genetic soundness and few Shibas are diagnosed with genetic defects in comparison to other dog breeds.

Life span

Their average life expectancy is from 12 to 15 years.

Grooming

These dogs are very clean, so grooming needs will likely be at a minimum for most individuals. A Shiba Inu coat is short, coarse and naturally waterproof, so there is little need for regular bathing. However, there is one drawback and that is shedding, also known as blowing coat. They have a thick undercoat that can protect them from temperatures well below freezing. Shedding is heaviest during the seasonal change, especially during the summer season, but brushing should be performed on a daily basis whenever possible.

See also

- Shiba Inu Puppy Cam

External links

- Shiba Inu [1] at the American Kennel Club website
- Shibas.org National Shiba Club of America [2]
- NYC Shiba Rescue [3]

Tibetan Spaniel

The **Tibetan Spaniel** is a breed of assertive, small, intelligent dogs originating in the Himalayan mountains of Tibet. They share ancestry with the Pekingese, Japanese Chin, Shih Tzu, Lhasa Apso, and Pug. This breed is not a true Spaniel; its breeding and role differs quite a bit (Spaniels are gun dogs.) The name Spaniel may have been given due to its resemblance to the bred-down lapdog versions of the hunting Spaniels, such as the Cavalier King Charles Spaniel.

Description

Appearance

The Tibetan Spaniel standard allows all colors, but with brown eyes and a black nose. Their temperament should be confident, active, and alert. The outline should give a well balanced appearance, slightly longer in body than the height at withers. The breed's height should be about 10 inches. The head should be slightly domed with a medium length, strong muzzle. The ideal weight is 9-15 pounds. The breed has a medium length double coat with flarings and a high set plumed tail, carried over their back.

Temperament

Tibetan spaniels are happy and assertive, highly intelligent dogs . "Tibbies", as they are often called, make excellent housepets for many people, including families with small children. Tibetan Spaniels enjoy attention and involvement with their owners, but have an independent nature and can be willful. They will bark to warn of strangers and strange occurrences, but are generally quiet.

Health Issues

Progressive Retinal Atrophy

Progressive retinal atrophy is a problem with this breed. The disease is an inherited form of blindness in dogs that occurs in two forms: generalized PRA and central PRA. Generalized PRA is primarily a photoreceptor disease and is the form found in Tibetan Spaniels. The clinical signs have been observed between 1½ and 4 years, but as late at seven years. The disease is painless and affected dogs become completely blind. Currently there is no treatment, but affected dogs generally adapt well to their progressive blindness.

The earliest clinical sign of progressive retinal atrophy is "night blindness." The dog cannot see well in a dimly lit room or at dusk. The dog will show a reluctance to move from a lighted area into darker surroundings. The night blindness develops progressively into complete blindness. The British institution Animal Health Trust (AHT) is at present intensively researching PRA in Tibetans Spaniels, aiming to isolate the responsible gene.

Liver Shunt - Portosystemic Shunt

A portosystemic shunt is an abnormal vessel that allows blood to bypass the liver, one of the body's filters, so that it is not cleansed. This condition is often referred to as a "liver shunt".

Most shunts cause recognizable symptoms by the time a dog is a young adult but are occasionally diagnosed only later in life. Since the severity of the condition can vary widely depending on how much blood flow is diverted past the liver it is possible for a lot of variation in clinical signs and time of onset. Often, this condition is recognized after a puppy fails to grow, allowing early diagnosis. Signs of portosystemic shunts include poor weight gain, sensitivity to sedatives (especially diazepam), depression, pushing the head against a solid object, seizures, weakness, salivation, vomiting, poor appetite, increased drinking and urinating, balance problems and frequent urinary tract disease or early onset of bladder stones. A dramatic increase of these signs after eating is a strong supportive sign of a portosystemic shunt.

Other Issues

Like many breeds of dog, Tibetan Spaniels are susceptible to allergies. They also tend to experience "cherry eye", a prolapsed third eyelid. The shape of a Tibetan Spaniel's face makes them prone to "weeping eye".

History

Small monastery dogs, thought to be early representatives of the Tibetan Spaniel, loyally trailed behind their Lama masters and came to be regarded as "little Lions" owing to their resemblance to the Chinese guardian lions that gave them great value and prestige. The practice of sending the dogs as gifts to the palaces of China and other Buddhist countries grew significantly, and more "lion dogs" were presented back to Tibet, continuing until as late as 1908. As a result of exchanges of Tibetan Spaniels between palaces and monasteries, the breed is likely to have common ancestors with Oriental breeds such as the Japanese Chin and the Pekingese.

Professor Ludvic von Schulmuth studied the origins of skeletal remains of dogs in human settlements as old as ten thousand years. The Professor created a genealogical tree of Tibetan dogs. It shows that the "Gobi Desert Kitchen Midden Dog", a small scavenger, evolved into the "Small Soft-Coated Drop-Eared Hunting Dog" which then evolved into the Tibetan Spaniel, Pekingese, and Japanese Chin. Intermixing of the Tibetan Spaniel with the Tibetan breeds Lhasa Apso and Shih Tzu resulted in both the latter breeds birthing the occasional "Prapso" - a pup with a shedding coat closely resembling the Tibetan Spaniel.

Legend has it that Tibbies were trained to turn the monks' prayer wheels, but it is more likely that their keen sight made them excellent monastery watchdogs, barking to warn of intruders and alert the monks.

Village-bred Tibetan Spaniels varied greatly in size and type, and the smaller puppies were usually given as gifts to the monasteries. In turn, these smaller dogs used in the monastery breeding programs were probably combined with the more elegant Tibetan Spaniel-type dogs brought from China. Those bred closer to the Chinese borders were characterized by shorter muzzles.

Not only was the Tibetan Spaniel prized as a pet and companion, it was considered a useful animal by all classes of Tibetans. During the day, the dogs would sit on the monastery walls keeping watch over the countryside below. Their keen eye, ability to see great distances, and alarm barking, made them good watchdogs. Modern-day Tibbies retain their ancestors' love of heights.

Tibetan Spaniels were being bred in the United Kingdom by the 1890s. The first authenticated reference we find to Tibetan Spaniels in the United States is a litter born out of two imported dogs from a Tibetan monastery in 1965. In January 1971, the Tibetan Spaniel Club of America was formed with 14 charter members. After a period in the Miscellaneous classes, the Tibetan Spaniel was accepted for AKC registration and became eligible to compete as a Non-Sporting breed effective January 1, 1984. The breed was recognized by the Fédération Cynologique Internationale in 1987, and placed in Group 9 Companion and Toy Dogs, Section 5 : Tibetan breeds.

See also

- Companion dog
- Companion Dog Group
- Toy Group
- Non-Sporting Group
- Utility Group
- Foo Dog, dog breeds originating in China that resemble Chinese guardian lions and hence are also called Foo or Fu Dogs or Lion Dogs.

References

- Miccio, Susan W. *The Tibetan Spaniel: A Gift From The Roof of the World*, OTR Publications, 1995. ISBN 0-940269-12-0

External links

- The Animal Health Trust website [1], containing more information on Progressive Retinal Atrophy
- Wanasea Tibetan Spaniels [2]
- Milestone Tibetan Spaniels [3]
- Tibbies.net [4]
- Tibetan Spaniel Club of America [5]

.

Tibetan Terrier

The **Tibetan Terrier** is not a member of the terrier group, the name being given to it by European travelers to Tibet who were reminded of terriers from back home when they first encountered the breed. Its origins are uncertain: Some sources claim them to be lucky temple dogs, whereas others place them as farm dogs.

The Tibetan Terrier is a dog with many uses, able to guard, herd, and also be a suitable companion dog. Their utility in Tibet meant that the first examples of the breed available in the west were generally given as gifts, as the Tibetan Terrier, along with other Tibetan breeds, were too valuable to the people who owned them to casually sell. As such, the early history of the breed is linked to only a handful of foundation dogs.

The Tibetan name for the breed, Tsang Apso, roughly translates to "shaggy or bearded (apso) dog, from the province of Tsang". Some old travelers' accounts give the name "Dokhi Apso," or "outdoor" Apso, indicating a working dog which lives outdoors. Other "Apso" dogs from Tibet include the smaller and more familiar Lhasa Apso (called the Lhasa Terrier in the early 1900s) and the very rare Do Khyi Apso (bearded Tibetan Mastiff, sometimes considered as a TT/TM cross.)

Recent DNA analysis has concluded that the Tibetan Terrier is descended from the most ancient dog breeds.

Description

History

The Tibetan Terrier - often called the Holy Dog of Tibet - has evolved over hundreds of years of harsh conditions, tempered by the warmth and care of monks high in the Himalayas. The "little people", as they were called, were highly valued as companions to the monks and families who owned them. They were treated like children in the family. Like the children, they eagerly assisted in taking care of the monastery's or family's property, their flocks and herds. Sure footed and reliable, they were sometimes sent to accompany a particularly esteemed traveler on a treacherous mountain journey home. No Tibetan in old Tibet who was fortunate enough to own a Tibetan Terrier would ever sell their dog. The dogs were considered good luck, and no one in their right mind would "sell" part of their luck. Mistreating or mismating a Tibetan Terrier could bring bad luck to the family and even the village. While they were not sold, they were given as gifts. The first Tibetan Terrier to come to Europe came with an English doctor who was given a dog in return for saving someone's life.

The Tibetan Terrier who has emerged from this special environment is a healthy, bouncy, well-proportioned breed with a gentle, fun temperament. He is highly intelligent, sensitive, and devoted. He is not a hunter, he may or may not be a herder. He is, above all, a companion. As a member of the family, he has few equals - constantly cheerful, wonderful with children, warm and affectionate. He is genuinely interested in your daily goings-on, will involve himself in your life and will soon take a position as a cherished member of your family. If you would like a companion who can think for himself or herself, "laugh" at you when you are wrong and make you laugh when you are sad - one that is beautiful to look at and has a very special history - come and meet a Tibetan Terrier. But be warned. You may never be free of their spell. "

Appearance

The appearance of the Tibetan Terrier is that of a powerful, medium sized dog of square proportions, with a shaggy coat. Overall, there should be a feel of balance. Fully grown, he or she should look like a miniaturized Old English Sheepdog.

The head is moderate, with a strong muzzle of medium length, and a skull neither rounded nor flat. The eyes are large, dark, and set fairly far apart. The V-shaped drop ears are well feathered, and should be set high on the sides of the skull. The nose is always black, regardless of coat colour.

The body is well muscled and compact. The length of the back should be equal to the height at the withers, giving the breed its typical square look. Height for either sex is 14-16 in (35–41 cm) and weight is 18-30 lb (8–14 kg), with 20-24 lb (9.5–11 kg) preferred, but all weights acceptable if in proportion to the size.

The tail is set high, well feathered, and carried in a curl over the back.

One of the more unusual features of the Tibetan Terrier is the broad, flat feet with hair between the toes. They are ideal for climbing mountains and act as natural snow shoes.

Coat

Tibetans have hair, not fur; as a result, their coat grows continuously and pet animals will require occasional trimming. They do not shed but rather slough hair at a rate similar to that of most humans. The exception is at approximately nine months when puppies slough their entire coat in advance of acquiring their adult coat. The double coat is profuse, with a warm undercoat and a topcoat which has the texture of human hair. It should not be silky or curled, but wavy is acceptable. Long and thick, it is shown natural, but should not be so long as to touch the floor, as is typical in breeds such as the Lhasa Apso or Maltese. A fall of hair covers the face and eyes, but long eyelashes generally prevent hair from getting in the Tibetan Terrier's eyes, and the breed has very good eyesight.

Color

All colors are permissible, barring liver and chocolate, and none are preferred. Tibetan Terriers are available in any combination of solid, particolor, tricolor, brindle or piebald, as long as the nose leather is black and the eyes and eye rims are dark. They also come in a golden colour

Temperament

The temperament has been one of the most attractive aspects of the breed since it was first established. They are amiable and affectionate family dogs, sensitive to their owners and gentle with older children. As is fitting a dog formerly used as a watch dog, they tend to be reserved around strangers, but should never be aggressive nor shy with them.

Suitable for apartment living, the Tibetan is still an energetic and surprisingly strong dog, and needs regular exercise. Their energy level and intelligence is well suited for dog sports such as agility. They are steadfast, determined, and clever, which can lead to them being stubborn. Some dogs of this breed can often be jealous, which can make it hard to live with another pet.

Though not yappy, the Tibetan Terrier has an assertive bark, likened to a rising siren.

Energy Level: moderate to high General Nature: happy, active, lively, intelligent, agile

- With Children: good if properly introduced, supervised with well behaved children
- With other pets: generally good
- With dogs: generally good
- Socialization requirements: required to help address inclination to shyness to strangers
- Ideal home characteristics: one devoted to regular grooming and care of the coat in addition to other needs
- Temperament Notes: charming and loyal, sensitive and intelligent
- Training requirement: dependent entirely on goals

- Intelligent and sensitive nature. Training kept interesting and positive will move quickly. This is not a dog that will benefit from force of any form.

Health

The Tibetan Terrier enjoys the long life span often associated with small dog breeds, and generally lives from 17–20 years.

Though an athletic breed that has been bred for a natural look, the Tibetan Terrier is still susceptible to a variety of health problems, especially those related to the eyes and joints. These can include:

- Canine hip dysplasia
- Luxating patella
- Progressive retinal atrophy
- Lens luxation
- Cataracts

Because of that, Tibetan Terrier clubs recommend purchasing from breeders who participate in eye and hip testing, such as the Canine Eye Registration Foundation (CERF) and Orthopedic Foundation for Animals (OFA).

Tibetans also have a history of being somewhat prone to allergies.

In addition, Tibetan Terriers carry the genetic disease Canine Neuronal Ceroid Lipofuscinosis, called "Batten Disease" in humans. Research is on-going to find the gene(s) responsible for this progressive disease in both TTs and humans.

See also

- Companion dog
- Companion Dog Group
- Utility Group
- Non-Sporting Group

Article Sources and Contributors

Breed Groups (dog) *Source*: http://en.wikipedia.org/?oldid=371298317 *Contributors*: 1 anonymous edits

American Kennel Club *Source*: http://en.wikipedia.org/?oldid=373448194 *Contributors*: 07bargem

Non-Sporting Group *Source*: http://en.wikipedia.org/?oldid=367706771 *Contributors*:

American Eskimo Dog *Source*: http://en.wikipedia.org/?oldid=376258186 *Contributors*: 1 anonymous edits

Bichon Frise *Source*: http://en.wikipedia.org/?oldid=376615223 *Contributors*:

Boston Terrier *Source*: http://en.wikipedia.org/?oldid=374480792 *Contributors*: GB fan

Bulldog *Source*: http://en.wikipedia.org/?oldid=376375195 *Contributors*: Dodo bird

Shar Pei *Source*: http://en.wikipedia.org/?oldid=373913305 *Contributors*:

Chow Chow *Source*: http://en.wikipedia.org/?oldid=375559069 *Contributors*: Zetawoof

Dalmatian (dog) *Source*: http://en.wikipedia.org/?oldid=375786052 *Contributors*: 1 anonymous edits

Finnish Spitz *Source*: http://en.wikipedia.org/?oldid=373682840 *Contributors*: Pitke

French Bulldog *Source*: http://en.wikipedia.org/?oldid=376549354 *Contributors*: 1 anonymous edits

Keeshond *Source*: http://en.wikipedia.org/?oldid=367658914 *Contributors*: PKT

Lhasa Apso *Source*: http://en.wikipedia.org/?oldid=374977440 *Contributors*: 1 anonymous edits

Löwchen *Source*: http://en.wikipedia.org/?oldid=364603855 *Contributors*: Auntof6

Poodle *Source*: http://en.wikipedia.org/?oldid=376462166 *Contributors*: Miyagawa

Schipperke *Source*: http://en.wikipedia.org/?oldid=375916156 *Contributors*: Slon02

Shiba Inu *Source*: http://en.wikipedia.org/?oldid=376157480 *Contributors*: Ohnoitsjamie

Tibetan Spaniel *Source*: http://en.wikipedia.org/?oldid=356177054 *Contributors*: GB fan

Tibetan Terrier *Source*: http://en.wikipedia.org/?oldid=374662386 *Contributors*: